Beyond Explanation?

BEYOND EXPLANATION?

*The Paranormal Experiences of
Famous People*

by

JENNY RANDLES

Salem House
Manchester, New Hampshire

© *Jenny Randles 1985*

First published in the United States by
Salem House Publishers, 1986
a member of the Merrimack Publishers' Circle
Manchester, New Hampshire 03101

ISBN: 0-88162-168-4

Library of Congress Catalog Card Number: 85-62525

Printed and bound in Great Britain

Contents

To the memory of Dr John Randall

Oh Doctor – Immortal man
How could you die?

Like a candle flame flickers and fades into dark

Like an actor who walks sadly from his part

But I will remember
How can I forget?

The deeds that you did will for ever live on

For time may pass
And man may pass

But good – that will always survive

Acknowledgements

For their help in my research to all the staff at *Fate* magazine in Illinois, the staff at Radio City, Liverpool. and the organization of the SPR for the work they have done.

To a very synchronistic and lovely city of Philadelphia (especially its railway station).

A special vote of thanks to ASSAP for the new ideas they are bringing to this field.

Individually I acknowledge the following for their information: Larry Arnold, Joe Keeton, Dick Kleiner, Ken and Ann Phillips, Gaynor and Marion Sunderland, Bill Tenuto, Nigel Watson and Rhys Williams.

And for their information and ideas I much respect the work of many, including: Rodney Jones, Dr Rupert Sheldrake, Dr Lyall Watson and Ian Watson.

Grateful appreciation is also due those writers, artists and (especially) musicians whose copyright I respect but whose words must be heard. But with an extra thank-you to Judith Starchild for her help and inspiration.

Finally, to all those I have omitted by accident – not forgetting John Lennon (who I guess might be righteously upset if I left him out!).

Introduction

Everyone loves a good story. It delights any party and almost guarantees you an escalation up the social ladder. Even more so, people love spooky tales of ghosts, things that go bump in the night, strange predictions and flying saucers.

There are many such anecdotes here. I hope they will provide interest and enjoyment, perhaps giving you the opportunity to do some yarn-spinning yourself. But added to this intention, I have a rather more serious purpose in mind.

The book has been built around famous people, celebrities from various walks of life, some from the past and some from today. This will hopefully offer an anchor for the strange and fantastic accounts that you will confront. It is all very well to be told that Mr Smith, of Anytown, saw a funny light in the sky one night, or that Mrs Jones, from Littleville, saw the ghost of her dead Aunt Mary. But these things mean precious little unless one happens to be a friend of Mr Smith or relative of Mrs Jones (or be her dead Aunt Mary for that matter!). It is all too easy to persuade yourself . . . well, it's only a book, these people are not real. You have no such escape from the stories I present here. You may try to dismiss their reality, but you cannot dismiss their story-tellers. Abraham Lincoln, Tommy Steele, John Lennon, Jules Verne and all the others in this book are actual people. The fact that they have undergone these alleged encounters somehow makes the stories seem all the more interesting and all the more 'true'.

There is another advantage of writing a book about weird phenomena from the viewpoint of famous people. I myself am an investigator of such things. In the broadest sense I suppose that means I believe that they can happen – which is not the same thing as believing that they always have happened, just because somebody says so. I pride myself on being reasonably sceptical. The popular ideas about the origin of a ghost, or a flying saucer, need not be the most likely explanation. Sometimes an answer can be found which is either more down to earth or, on occasions, even more amazing than the one we might expect. It is this which makes the hunt for anomalies so exciting. One has to play detective, taking statements, finding clues, putting together a complex jigsaw and then finally reaching a decision. What really did happen at two o'clock that morning when a white spectral mass briefly appeared by Colonel So and So's bedside?

That is what ASSAP (the Association for the Scientific Study of Anomalous Phenomena) is all about. I enjoy my work with them, as do many others. But above all I realize that it is not just a game. A good many people undergo anomalous experiences and emerge frightened or bemused, without any idea of where they can turn. Their neighbours laugh. Their family feels sorry for them. The police listen carefully and then file the report in their 'crackpot file', which usually doubles as the wastebin! And scientists, or the many self-professed media experts, will tell you that what you saw could not have happened; it is an impossibility.

Imagine yourself the confused victim of such a circumstance. I know from my dozen years' investigation that many of you reading this book will be such victims, just as some of you will turn to it for pure entertainment. The number of people who believe they have had an encounter with the paranormal is astonishingly high. Upwards of fifty per cent of the population have probably faced a situation which common sense simply cannot explain. I know that I have had my own minor intrusions into some of the subjects we shall delve into. And there is nothing peculiar about that. I tend to feel that most of us meet the paranormal head on without realizing that we have done so. Yet those 'experts' (who are in the minority and have generally never faced the problem first-hand) will continue to tell us that our eyesight was defective, or we fell asleep without knowing it, or (if they are a bit less kind than most of their peers) suggest we were drunk or are a 'fantasy-prone character'. This latter is their way of stating we are crackers! The honest truth is that a lot of witnesses to strange phenomena are *none* of these things. They are simple, honest, reliable folk who have genuinely observed something under dependable circumstances which all their past experience tells them cannot be.

When the impossible happens, it is a shock to the system. You find yourself questioning more than just your sanity. You may even doubt that the world as you know it is the world as it truly must be.

Our society has a problem dealing with these strange anomalies. It tries hard to pretend that they are not there. But the totality of our history proves that this is a false and dangerous illusion. We are missing out on some pretty interesting things, and perhaps even some pretty important things. You can never make an unwanted problem disappear by casting magic spells. Problems are resolved only by thinking them through. And to do that you must first acknowledge that they exist.

I have tried to think these problems through, and I do suggest some ideas about their possible solution, but I do not expect you to take my word at face value. I am forced to trust the word of witnesses, for sometimes the theories I build stand or fall on their integrity. So you must challenge what I say and think things through for yourself. In the end it is the only true way to illumination. As I once put it, 'All the answers to your questions only you can find.'

Millions of people, without exaggeration, have undergone the sort of experiences you will read of in this book. Many of them have told almost nobody (perhaps even nobody) about what took place. They do this for fear of ridicule, or damage to their social status, or in the belief that the TV prophets must be right if they say that such a thing cannot occur. This book is a sort of mental fillip for such unfortunates. It is an ego-boost and an aid to morale. To learn that the famous with whom we all share our lives are human and fallible just like ourselves is in itself pleasant, but to be told that they too face the unknown and then have the courage to say so is perhaps a lesson well worth contemplating. And it will certainly be encouraging for those who have recently had a strange experience to discover that these things do not always wreck your life, act as a presage to mental collapse or signal disaster and death. Often they can be illuminating and have produced great inventions and wonderful creative masterpieces or have acted as warnings to prevent life-threatening or unpleasant situations from coming to pass.

The paranormal is not something to be scared of. We should not view it in the way that an aborigine once viewed the overflying aircraft – as a wicked or terrifying phantom. Instead it is a marvellous and exciting facet of human life. The one thing it does prove is that we are incredible creatures, with depths undreamt of there to explore, depths vaster than the oceans of this world, or of space – yet depths which we know so little about. One day mankind will realize that, for much less money than the cost of one rocketship, we could visit an amazing universe which is so close at hand that we take it all for granted. That universe lies within us. It is the universe of man.

Read these tales with interest and amusement, but also with awe, for the emotions they inspire can be each of these things. However, please do not forget as you turn the pages that what your favourite movie star, comedian or entertainer is claiming is but one example of thousands of experiences very much like it. It is one grain of sand amidst the Sahara.

Remember that such things can happen to both famous and ordinary folk alike, that it matters not if you are a dustman or a duchess, a printer or a president, a milkman or a millionaire. This is the real wonder of our great mysterious world. One day – and it could be today – you may be the person who dreams the future before it happens, or who wakes to find a strange, eerie visitor beside your bed. You will then become the next grain of sand within that desert. When it happens, this book may help you face the consequences with calm anticipation, for you will have just broken through the tissued veil which stands between what you once called the 'real' world and the land of illusions.

At last you will realize the true meaning of the words 'Nothing is impossible'. For nothing is . . . well, almost nothing.

1. The Other Side of Famous Folk

'If I had to live all over again, I should devote myself to
psychical research' – Sigmund Freud.

'Holmes – something has secreted itself beneath this mushroom.'

The Detective stooped to inspect the matter and then rose
again, nodding briefly and puffing once on his pipe.

'Watson – I deduce it was a small creature, height
approximately four inches, with a body substance light and
ethereal, wearing a flimsy, gossamer dress and blessed with
wings of heavenly perfection.'

'Are you saying . . .?'

'Yes, indeed . . . it was a fairy.'

Dr Watson faced his colleague staunchly, hands on hips, and
spluttered faintly into the dawn breeze. 'But . . . how could you
possibly know that, Holmes?'

'Elementally, my dear Watson. Elementally.'

This invented whimsical passage from the works of the great
writer Arthur Conan Doyle, the man who created Sherlock
Holmes, portrays a point, for Conan Doyle, despite his brilliance
at writing fiction, was a man who had a deep and abiding interest
in all things paranormal. Some would call him open-minded,
others just plain gullible (certainly we know that he was taken in
by one of the biggest deceptions of the twentieth century), for
Conan Doyle actively promoted the existence of various kinds of

other-worldly creatures (or elementals as they are known). In particular he believed in fairies.

Conan Doyle was a very adventurous fellow, not unlike his character Professor Challenger. With his literary colleague Robert Louis Stevenson, he joined the Society for Psychical Research. Indeed the two used to write to one another with the address, 'Dear Fellow Spookhunter'! Whilst Conan Doyle did not regard himself as a psychic, he certainly had flashes of intuition about the future, which he used to good effect in writing his stories. (In 1913 he penned *Danger*, which accurately described the German U-boat threat in the coming war.) Stevenson was not without such talents. He created his classic tale *Dr Jekyll and Mr Hyde* out of a particularly vivid dream which came when he was searching for a way to express the idea's basic moral. He could recall it all perfectly, and the results are self-explanatory. (We shall return to this interesting common ability of writers later in the book.)

Eventually Conan Doyle gave up his fiction entirely (much to the disappointment of his many fans). He then pursued something of a personal crusade, lecturing and writing on the perceived reality of life after death. For him this was to be his ultimate purpose, but it is sad that he will not be best remembered for these laudable escapades in the world of the paranormal. Instead people will think of the time in 1920 when he was writing an article for *Strand* magazine, eventually entitled 'The Fairies Photographed'.

In his first draft of this article Conan Doyle proposed his belief in such creatures, but said he had no proof. Then, by chance, he discovered some pictures taken by two teenaged girls, Elsie Wright and Frances Griffiths, in a dell at Cottingley, West Yorkshire. These not only changed the title of his article: they changed his life.

The photographs depict the girls playing with fairies and gnomes amidst trees and grass. Five in all were taken. However, 'convincing' is the last word appropriate to them. The fairies look like cardboard cut-outs, and in at least one shot the creature which forms the centrepiece of the picture is being totally ignored by Frances, in favour of gaping at the camera lens! The official 'explanation' for this was that the girls had seen many fairies – but a camera: now that was something much more interesting! Conan Doyle wanted the pictures to be genuine, and he failed to spot any of the problems associated with them. Nor did he worry when the girls miserably failed to repeat their spectacular results during future attempts in the dell, despite their insistence that it was always full of fairies. Skipping the hurdles, Conan Doyle pronounced the photographs conclusive evidence and expanded his article into a book, *The Coming of the Fairies*, which not surprisingly sold rather well.

Sadly for Conan Doyle, and all fairy-lovers, these photographs (which became famed throughout the world) are precisely the fakes which first glance makes one suspect. Elsie and Frances laughed silently at us all for sixty years as the evidence slowly mounted against them. Elsie's artistic talents were well known, and the 1917 style of hair worn by the elementals always seemed rather more likely to have emerged from her pen than from the land of Magonia. Eventually the book from which this and the other fairies were copied was discovered. Computer enhancement techniques, born of the Space Age, were also employed by a group normally interested in the analysis of UFO pictures. The results were damning. The fairies were two-dimensional (not even three, let alone four!), and there were clear signs of fabrication. The cumulative verdict was unequivocal. They were fakes.

In 1975 Elsie was tracked down by a TV reporter and gave her first interview in years. Faced with the growing evidence, she said that the pictures were 'photographs of figments of our imagination'. That sounds fair enough, but when pressed to clarify this ambiguous remark she still insisted the pictures were real. Only several years later did Elsie finally confess to the hoax, and when Frances was interviewed she agreed. However, both were adamant that they really had seen fairies in the dell – and Frances even (inexplicably) says that only four out of the five pictures are fake. One of them is genuine!

The way Arthur Conan Doyle, undoubtedly a clever and imaginative man, could totally submit to his beliefs and ignore the normal scientific standards of evidence (with which he was familiar from his medical training) sounds a warning bell to all who become entrapped in the world of strange phenomena. That modern-day researchers at least try to be more objective is shown by the way their combined efforts eventually chipped away the crumbling evidence bit by bit. Surely this is better than the establishment science attitude, well demonstrated by photographic analysts from Kodak, who were asked to pronounce on the status of the images when Doyle was first touting them. Kodak stated that they obviously could not be pictures of fairies, for the eminently scientific reason that there are no fairies to take any pictures of!

I would like to think that Doyle would welcome any attempt to set the record straight and frankly admit he had made rather an ass of himself. Otherwise Holmes would have been most disappointed in him.

Arthur Conan Doyle and Robert Louis Stevenson were by no means the only famous people to participate in the early years of the SPR (Society for Psychical Research). Indeed the Society membership lists often read like a veritable *Who's Who* of those days.

The SPR set up operations in 1882, after a wave of table-turning and Spiritualism began to sweep through Britain. The pioneers, including the famous physicist Sir William Barrett and brilliant classical scholar Frederick Myers, were determined to bring scientific principles to bear on the investigation of such phenomena. Over the next century these men and their successors attracted to the cause such a diversity of talent that anybody who wishes to regard students of the paranormal as 'weird' is going to have to revise his views of an awful lot of respected people. In science there have been many, from physicists such as Sir Oliver Lodge and Sir William Crookes, through astronomers (Camille Flammarion) to Nobel Prize winning physiologist Charles Richet. There have been philosophers and psychologists (such as Henri Bergson and William James). There have even been Prime Ministers, including Lord Balfour (who ran the country between 1902 and 1906 at about the same time as he served as President of the SPR). Imagine such a move today! Maggie Thatcher – ghost-hunter: I think not!

But the SPR is not a society of the past. Today it still attracts a diversity and has active and renowned scientists in the fields of mathematics, physics, biology etc. Its achievement is best illustrated by the fact that some universities now have parapsychologists on their staff (this is the name the scientists give themselves to help become accepted among their peers). Indeed, the philosopher Arthur Koestler, another SPR adherent, left a million pounds in his will, and in 1984 this was used to set up a full-time research department at Edinburgh University, applying SPR guidelines.

A century after its foundation, the Society has not proved its case, but it is trying ever more convoluted means to do so. Its scientific experiments have kept pace with the growth of modern technology, and the current crop of researchers, such as Dr Julian Isaacs and Dr Carl Sargeant, use computers and electronics to seek out the basis of telepathy (mind-to-mind communication) and psychokinesis (the moving of objects by apparently non-physical means).

This work is splendid and vital. I have been an SPR member myself (but no longer am) and I support its basic aims as far as is practicable. The problem is that the Society bends over backwards to be scientific. Not that there is anything very wrong with that, but it allows its members to concentrate on only fairly dry areas, such as those mentioned. Relatively little effort is applied to spontaneous anomalies. In some real respects the SPR is not in touch with the needs and experiences of ordinary individuals who face the world of the paranormal.

It was this thinking that lay behind the creation of ASSAP (the Association for the Scientific Study of Anomalous Phenomena), formed as a sort of break-away offshoot from the SPR in 1981. ASSAP certainly regards its role and that of its 'parent' as mutually compatible, and it aims to concentrate on both a wider diversity of phenomena (recognizing that there may be useful inter-relationships to be found) and also to devote its attention to spontaneous experiences (such as apparitions, time-slips, premonitions and so forth). No scientific training is required to be an ASSAP field investigator, although in-service training is a key feature, and certain principles of scientific investigation are required (including a code of ethics).

Two other names to feature in the annals of SPR history are perhaps the best-known 'mind scientists' of the twentieth century. They are men who have shaped the whole pattern of current thinking in this area: Sigmund Freud and Carl Jung.

Freud, the pioneer of psychoanalysis and the dream-interpretation, was *not* a fan of what he called 'the occult'. Indeed he tended to bemoan those who, he argued, went with 'the black tide of mud of occultism'. But he did have an on/off love-affair with telepathy, and he joined the SPR to further his study of the phenomenon. He never became totally persuaded by the evidence, but a few experiences with his patients teased him sufficiently to keep the mind open. For example, he recorded an instance where one patient alleged that a fortune-teller had offered a reading about a friend, stating he would die that summer from eating poisoned shellfish. In fact, the man had almost died from this effect and such information was therefore somewhere in his subconscious mind at the time of the 'reading'. Freud interpreted the 'prediction' as more probably a 'telepathic message' between fortune-teller and client.

In fact, despite his ambivalence about the matter, Freud was himself concerned enough over the relationship between telepathy and prediction seriously to wonder if some discussions and plans he had innocently made about his father's future death had been responsible when a few months later the old man became critically ill. Freud's father was eighty-one at the time, so you might regard this as a strange attitude, but Freud wrote, 'Certain things should not even be mentioned in jest, otherwise they come true.'

Carl Gustav Jung, born in Switzerland, became the most imaginative psychological theorizer of the twentieth century. Unlike Freud's, his life was steeped in strange phenomena, and he became an outspoken supporter of telepathy, precognition and (to many people's surprise) astrology.

Jung's family had a history of peculiar goings-on. His mother regularly recorded her own precognitions, and the many 'coincidences' which occurred during her life helped to fuel her son's passionate concern. In 1898 two dramatic examples of psychokinesis at home were recorded, both accompanied by loud bangs, like gunshots. In the first instance Jung and his mother found a walnut table split right open. In the other the sound seemed to emerge from a sideboard, which was discovered to contain a knife shattered into four pieces. These events have much in common with what today we would call 'poltergeist outbreaks'; both are regarded by serious researchers as uncontrolled bursts of the mysterious PK (psychokinetic) energy. As his mother was present on both occasions (and Jung was not), it seems likely that she was the focus through which the energy was externalized, but Jung's role can hardly have been incidental.

In 1907 Jung met Freud and they became close friends, although they disagreed on much (and later fell out). In 1909 Jung went to Vienna to see his colleague, and they discussed the paranormal. Jung related the broken knife incident, to which

Freud merely replied 'Bosh!' Before Jung could formulate a conscious reply, his subconscious may have acted for him. He says that his anger grew to a 'curious sensation' in his diaphragm, as if it were 'made of iron and becoming red hot'. There was an eerie loud 'explosion' from Freud's bookcase across the room. Jung commented that it would probably happen again, and moments later it did. No longer would Freud denigrate paranormal. Instead he reacted in the other typical fashion of the establishment scientist, preferring not to talk about the matter at all.

Jung went on to develop his far-seeing ideas about psychological complexes, extroverts and introverts, and the collective unconscious. Through this he began to search for 'archetypes' within human society which he believed were powerful driving influences in unconscious thought (and thus behaviour). To do this he extensively studied myths, magic and psychic phenomena, occasionally witnessing events he himself considered genuine. He had a strange vision about the city of Liverpool (in which he saw it as a reflection of the term 'pool of life'), and he also seems to have detected the horrific emotional intensity of World War I, before it happened – thus generating a sort of premonition of its coming terrors. Two years before he died, in 1959, he even published one of the most perceptive books on UFOs – such was the breadth of his thinking.

Jung came together with a famous physicist, Dr Wolfgang Pauli, to create an elaborate theory known as 'synchronicity'. Through this he sought to explain that all events relate to one another across time and space. He regarded the mind as the principal causation of what later appears to be coincidence, and he saw in this a way of explaining astrology, the ancient superstition which he had taken to his heart and treated as a science. Pauli, as a father of the sub-atomic physics known as 'Quantum Mechanics', was wrestling with baffling mysteries that still beset the subject today. He could envisage the mind (or, more appropriately, consciousness in general) as the missing variable in all the equations which were just not working out otherwise. What is born or done at a certain moment has all the characteristics of that moment in time, was the poetic way in which Carl Jung expressed his ideas.

Although this might seem like another great man subsuming himself to mystery and superstition, it is perhaps opportune to point out that astrology does have some claim to being a 'science' – if nothing else, because of the length of time it has persisted and the number of ancient cultures which 'invented' it. For most of the history of civilization it has been at one with astronomy and cosmology, and every famous person in such fields was also (indeed, often primarily) an astrologer. From Ptolemy to Tycho Brahe and including one of England's most famous sons, Sir Isaac Newton, they have all studied and used the subject in their work and continued to believe in its efficacy. They did this not out of blind delusion, as most modern scientists assume, but because they had tested it in practice and found it to be valid. These men challenged the most basic beliefs of mankind and substituted brave new hypotheses. Would they really be foolish enough to perpetuate a nonsense? Newton himself summed up the position when he was asked why, in the days of scientific renaissance, he could lend his support to the fallacy of astrology. 'Sir,' he is said to have replied, 'I have studied it. You have not.'

Already we have met with astrology, prediction, psychokinesis and elemental beings in our introductory trek through the great names of the past. But literally every sort of strange phenomenon has been shared by the famous, both then and now. Let us skip through a potpourri of tales in rough chronological (but no other particular) order. On the way I will point out a few things which we will come back to in more detail later in the book.

Charles Dickens demonstrated the hold which mysteries have on our minds. He often delved into little anecdotes of strange phenomena and wrote stories around them. Indeed, he was personally fascinated by the enigma of spontaneous human combustion and was one of the earliest authorities with an extensive knowledge of the matter. In his novel *Bleak House* he deliberately allowed the appropriately named villain, Krook, to die in this way – and he based the event on real-life episodes.

Nobody knows even today what spontaneous human combustion is. But there are now many reliable case-histories, with grim photographic evidence to support its reality. Typically the victim just catches fire, for no obvious reason, and burns from the inside out, often with a bluish flame. Eye-witnesses who have seen the phenomenon attest that the flame cannot be extinguished and the body is rapidly consumed. Since incredible heat is required to turn bone into ash, one quickly sees the difficulty of the problem. Blaze investigators discover that the damage is always localized – indeed, it is this fact which draws attention to the mystery in the first place. The victim's remains (which may be just one leg astride a pile of ash!) lie in a heap, but the surrounding furniture and carpets are virtually untouched. Clearly the intense heat from the destruction of the body ought to do far more damage than this, if not burn the entire house down.

Larry Arnold, one of the world's leading researchers in this phenomenon, told me that fire chiefs and doctors usually refuse to acknowledge that spontaneous combustion truly occurs. But his files of testimony and explicit pictures demonstrate beyond doubt that it seems to happen more often than we realize. Such a refusal to admit the existence of a problem that seems insoluble is sadly very commonplace. Theories as to what actually occurs during spontaneous human combustion range from the sudden formation of ball lightning within a person's body, or a dramatic flip in its chemical balance, to microwave radiation generated by changes in the electromagnetic field strength within the victim. Whatever the truth of this bizarre and fortunately rare phenomenon, we shall probably have ultimately to recognize Charles Dickens was one of its first proponents.

Dickens contributed a further relevant little tale. His image of the ghost of Marley appearing to Scrooge in *A Christmas Carol* is perhaps one of the most dramatic visual creations of a writer. The clanking ball and the chain which tethers the ghost in most illustrative reproductions of the scene are not based on real experience. No ghosts ever appear with such impedances. But it is a sort of pictorial reflection of a cultural belief about ghosts, as prevalent now as it was in the last century. The ghost is considered by many to be a dead spirit who has somehow become shackled to the earthplane and who cannot escape to the higher dimensions of life after death. Hence the ball and chain, as a convenient analogy of this 'imprisonment'. In fact, Charles Dickens may well have had the last laugh on all of us. In Chapter 12 we shall consider his very strange 'return' from the 'world beyond the grave'.

Sam Clemens may well be regarded as America's Charles Dickens, although he will be better known to you by his *nom-de-plume*, Mark Twain. Before he became a novelist, he worked with his brother Henry on a steamboat which plied the Mississippi, and it was here that he came face to face with the unexplained.

Sam had an argument with his boss and was transferred off the ship to another one, but Henry remained behind. Whilst on shore during a visit, Sam then had a vivid and terrible dream, in which he saw his brother in a coffin laid across two chairs. On his chest was a bunch of white flowers with one central red rose. Henry's boat set off down river, and Sam's followed a little later. Upon arrival in port he received the news that his former steamship had blown apart, killing 150 people. Henry had survived but was fatally wounded. Six days later Sam watched by his brother's bedside, until Henry succumbed. Exhausted and in grief, he fell asleep, only to awaken to find the scene as it had been in his dream. The flowers were the only thing missing, but a woman was stepping up to the body and placing on it a bunch of white blooms and one central red rose.

Such vivid precognitive dreams are note at all rare. Movie star David Janssen, who was 'The Fugitive' in the famous TV series of that name, had a most disturbing one. He saw himself being carried out in a coffin, and when he asked in the dream what had happened, he was told that David Janssen had suffered a heart attack. He was sufficiently upset to approach a local psychic for advice, and she told him to take a medical check. Unfortunately it was too late. Two days later, a massive heart attack did kill him.

We shall meet many other, similar examples throughout this book, and it is my contention that we *all* experience dreams of the future on a fairly regular basis. I say this from personal experience and experiment, which, it is only fair I make plain, has to my satisfaction entirely demonstrated the reality of this particular kind of anomaly.

However, it is worth recording one other experience which Sam Clemens/Mark Twain described. He was idly watching a man approach a nearby house when suddenly (within a blink) that man vanished. It sounds like a ghost story, but it is not, for, unlike many who may have experienced this and then presumed the strange man to be a phantom, Clemens went to the house and checked. Sure enough the man was inside. He had just not been seen entering. What had actually occurred was that Clemens had undergone a brief 'time lapse', perhaps of just a few seconds or maybe a few minutes, during which he was unconscious. When he regained consciousness, he was still standing where he was before, so the only thing which had changed in the external world was the appearance/disappearance of the man, and Sam Clemens had no way of knowing that he had suffered this odd malady.

Such a remarkable experience is actually old hat to the modern UFO investigator. A good parallel is the case of West Yorkshire police officer Alan Godfrey. He was driving in search of some straying cattle on an early morning in November 1980 when he came across a strange object straddling the road. After he had sketched the 'UFO', it vanished, within a blink, and only the fact that Alan now seemed to be a little further down the road than he was previously suggested that something had occurred of which he had no memory. However, he was tempted to ignore the time-factor mystery until careful reconstruction indicated that as much as fifteen minutes had disappeared from his recall.

In the modern UFO world there is now a ready-made way out of this difficulty. The witness is generally subjected to regression hypnosis, led back to recall the incident and go on to retrieve (or create) a memory (or fantasy) of what took place in the blank period. It almost always involves abduction by strange alien creatures of a remarkably banal and anthropomorphic nature. And unfortunately nobody has any idea if it is memory, fantasy or a mixture of the two. However, are we to suppose that Mark Twain is the first man in history ever abducted by aliens? Surely not!

The truth is that the writer was diagnosed as suffering from an interesting condition known as narcolepsy. Narcoleptics can sleep for brief periods during the course of normal behaviour, and they do not realize they have done so. I should add that at least one psychologist (without examining Alan Godfrey) explained his time lapse (although not, of course, the original UFO) in this way. But Godfrey has been examined by more than half a dozen psychiatrists and psychologists and, apart from the secondary evidence of several previous 'time lapses' in his younger life, absolutely no sign of narcolepsy was found.

Certain types of epileptic seizure have effects similar to this, as indeed does sleep-walking. A friend who used to suffer badly from this relates how one night he got out of bed in his sleep, went downstairs, put on the hi-fi at top volume and proceeded to disco-dance on the living-room floor! He was rapidly led back to bed. I hasten to add that he has no memory of these events whatsoever, the story being relayed by his somewhat embarrassed wife.

All we can reasonably conclude from these things is that the individual enters a different state of consciousness during the UFO abduction/narcoleptic or epileptic/sleep-walking incident. If consciousness is functioning at any level amidst the experience, it may be the source of the images later recalled. Although what these images are and why they originate is another matter altogether, I believe this to be an extreme example of what I call the 'Quasi-Conscious Experience' (or QC Experience for short). The end product is not conscious everyday experience and not subconscious fantasy as such. It is something else in between.

Talk of UFOs brings us round to the brush with the paranormal reported by TV star Hughie Green, perhaps best known for his *Opportunity Knocks* talent show. He was a flight major in the RAF just after World War II and in early July 1947 was driving to Philadelphia through the New Mexico desert when he heard some very curious reports on his car radio. These told that a 'flying disc' (the term UFO had yet to be invented) had crashed and was being recovered by the authorities. Several updates were offered, and Hughie was most intrigued because of his flying background and wartime experience of 'foo-fighters', as the UFOs of that era were called. Upon reaching his destination, the Flight Major was puzzled to find that no newspaper or radio station carried the big story, so he asked some media friends, who said that they had heard a few whispers, but a clamp had been put on the incident.

On its own the claim means little, but the rumour has been followed up by UFO investigators, such as Bill Moore of the Citizens Against UFO Secrecy organization. This uncovered alleged eye-witness testimony of the events which, backed by newspaper articles at the time in the Roswell, New Mexico, area, do suggest that a strange metallic object was indeed recovered. A press release to this effect seems to have been issued in haste and in error. Then the upper echelons of the US government decreed that a secrecy ban must be placed on it, and a cover-story was offered to the press, saying that the object was a weather balloon. Meanwhile that 'weather balloon' seems to have been put on board a special transport plane bound for a military research establishment.

Oblique confirmation comes in the form of documents released by the Freedom of Information Act in 1976. A memo dated 15 July

1947 (a few days after these events) is one of the most remarkable. It was an internal FBI communication discussing a request by the US authorities that the bureau assist the army/air force in recovery of and investigation work on 'UFOs', because, quote, 'It has been established that the flying discs are not the result of any Army (air force) or navy experiments. . . .' Appended to this memo was a fascinating comment by J. Edgar Hoover, the famous head of the FBI, saying, 'I would do it, but before agreeing to it we must insist upon full access to discs recovered . . .'; he adds, most provocatively, that in a recent case (which may possibly have been the one at Roswell), 'The army (air force) grabbed it and would not let us have it for cursory examination.'

Later the FBI went on to insist publicly that they never had any interest in UFO reports, but this intriguing memo and numerous subsequent papers prove decisively otherwise. Indeed, such papers reveal that the FBI gave up working on UFO cases because Hoover grew tired of having to deal with all the uninteresting cases whilst the other authorities were given jurisdiction over the truly important ones!

In December 1980 a very similar drama was played out in Rendlesham Forest, Suffolk, and once more some sort of cover-story seems to have been invented. The passage of three decades has altered matters very little.

I will close this chapter with a most remarkable story told by that vivacious singer and entertainer Tommy Steele. It is the sort of case to shake anybody's reservations about the unknown.

At fifteen Tommy ran away to sea, but he had been in the merchant navy only a few months when he was taken very ill. The doctor on the liner on which he served was so worried that he had him flown back to Britain, where, in a London hospital, spinal meningitis was diagnosed. The prognosis was very poor. By the time Tommy's parents reached his bedside, the belief was that he would not survive the night.

However, survive he did. The next morning he was breathing but still in a critical condition, totally paralysed below the waist and on doctors' advice his parents left him alone for a while to continue his fight for breath. As Tommy lay there, he became aware firstly of a child's laughter and then of a brightly coloured ball which bounced over the screens set up around him. The ball landed on his bed, and Tommy somehow summoned up the strength to stretch out and grab it, throwing it back to the child beyond the screen. He then fell back onto the pillow exhausted. A few minutes later it happened again. This time the ball landed a little further away. But Tommy has always loved children (as is evident from his many delightful movies – such as *Half a Sixpence*), and with supreme effort he retrieved it again and threw it back to the still laughing child. During the next few hours this repeated itself several times, and Tommy slowly found his strength returning. Eventually he was able to make tentative steps out of bed, and after this the ball stopped sailing over. Shortly after that the doctor and his parents returned and were astonished at the improvement. The fever and paralysis were subsiding. Tommy was well on the road to recovery.

The doctor shook his head, unable to comprehend what had happened, but Tommy merely explained that they should all thank the child across the ward. Without the exercise and effort in retrieving the ball, he would not have got better. Nonplussed, they removed the screens. There was no boy. Nor had there ever been. But when Tommy described the ball, his parents looked at one another and reminded their son about his younger brother, Rodney. Several years before, Rodney had died tragically, whilst only three years old. His favourite toy had been a rubber ball, exactly like that which Tommy had just observed. In fact, Tommy had given the ball to Rodney as a present on his very last Christmas.

Had Tommy Steele's subconscious mind, whilst in a fever of delirium, used these facts buried in his memory to construct a fantastic illusion that would force the teenager to cure himself? This is the sort of answer a modern parapsychologist would probably suggest. But a sustained illusion of this depth would be quite a feat. Of course, the only alternative is even more amazing. Did Rodney return from death and save the life of his brother, so as to allow him to go on to bring much joy and pleasure to millions of other children in the years to come? Such an idea has the kind of delightful excitement which the world of strange phenomena is really all about. And the need to make such a very intriguing choice sums up the challenge which this book will lay down.

2. Strange Tricks of Fate

'Let us learn how to dream. . . and then perhaps we will
discover the truth' – Friedrich von Kekulé (chemist).

I remember a story told to me by some close friends a few years
ago. They were a young couple not prone to hyper-imagination
and with feet very firmly on the ground.

While they were engaged to be married, the young woman had
developed symptoms that both suspected could involve a rather
unexpected and unwelcome pregnancy. A test was carried out,
but it proved to be negative. However, circumstances were conspiring so that they were unable to forget their convictions.
Everywhere they went, babies figured in their lives: women with
prams would run into them in the streets; each shop they entered
would be filled with babbling tiny tots; if they visited a relative or
acquaintance, a caller would arrive at the same time to show off
their latest family addition. My friends could not escape from the
belief that someone, somewhere, was trying to tell them something. Further tests were conducted but absolutely confirmed
that there was no pregnancy. And only then, as they made firm
resolutions to accept this fact, did the odd coincidences stop. Of
course, I realize that they might have been guilty of selective
attention – taking more note of baby situations because of the
circumstances – but they are persuaded otherwise. Both feel the
phenomenon was real.

If they are correct, it would almost seem that a sort of intricate
link was opened up between this couple and the world around

them. Their thoughts and fears became translated into real events – producing a sort of conspiracy that constantly manoeuvred them into the right place at the right time. In this way a warning was served.

In July 1900 King Umberto I of Italy found himself in a similar situation. Only for him the outcome was far less uneventful.

Dining one evening in a restaurant, he became fascinated by the owner, who bore a striking physical resemblance to the King. Indeed the two men even shared the same name. Upon his questioning the man, the weird links between them developed to an astounding level. They had been born on the same day, in the same town, and they had even married women with the same name.

This is an example of what are known as 'time twins'. Astrologers – and Carl Jung, as you will recall – argue that everything 'born' at a certain time and place becomes imprinted with the characteristics of that time and place. In the same way, as biological twins (who, of course, are naturally born close together in time and space) often go on to lead similar lives, so too may 'time twins', even when there is no genetic relationship at all.

Patricia Kern (of Colorado) and Patricia di Biasi (of Oregon) discovered this truth when a mix-up in a computer gave them the same social security number. This resulted in the two coming together during 1984. Both women had been born Patricia Ann Campbell, with fathers named Robert. Both have worked as book-keepers, have studied cosmetics and love to paint using oils. Both married military men (within eleven days of one another in 1959). Both have children aged twenty-one and nineteen. And, of course, the two entirely unrelated women were both born on 13 March 1941. Such a curious state of affairs is not at all rare. Were you to search hard enough for another person born geographically close to yourself on the same day, you might be surprised at the similarities in your lives. The effect is even sometimes noticeable when the year separating the two people is different (but the date is the same). I hardly need point out the comparisons in the example of famous horror-movie actors Vincent Price and Peter Cushing who demonstrate this situation.

And so it was with King Umberto and the restaurant owner. They came to share a very special relationship – so special that the King invited his 'twin' to be his guest at the athletics meeting which he was due to attend the next day. But the man failed to arrive. The King was very disappointed and made inquiries as to why his new-found friend had not turned up. An attendant reported that the man had died that very morning in a shooting incident. Soon after the King received this tragic news, an assassin stepped from the crowd, levelled a gun and shot him dead. The lives of the 'time twins' had run together to the end.

Astrology, as such, is not an explanation for this phenomenon, for it is merely a description of circumstances and carries no convincing over-all theory. It is one facet of the universe in its real, fundamental state which we as yet do not fully comprehend. The actual solution to the sad death of King Umberto and his 'twin', and to my friends' protracted encounter with babies, lies in an intangible something which serves as a co-ordinating influence in the cosmos. Carl Jung and Wolfgang Pauli labelled it 'synchronicity', if you recall. There have been other theories with other names, but one might just as well refer to it as 'God'.

'Tricks of fate', another way of expressing the principle, often effect the lives of famous people. Consider the experience of Hollywood actor Robert Stack. He had gone through an exciting but unspectacular film career which had produced a small degree of success but not the great breakthrough he was hoping for. When he was offered the part of gang-buster 'Elliot Ness' in a pilot show for TV entitled *The Untouchables*, he had just emerged from a costly movie failure which he had been convinced was going to make him a star, so he was not inclined to jump into the first part offered, especially when he asked around and discovered that the general opinion of those informed about such matters was that *The Untouchables* was sure to be a flop. He then learnt that two other actors had turned the part down, including the veteran Van Heflin, and that he had just a couple of days to make up his mind before shooting began. So he rejected it. But something nagged at Robert Stack. Perhaps this *was* the part. Maybe he ought to take it. He tried to consult a psychic whom his wife knew and whose advice he greatly respected. By the time he did contact her (and she suggested that he *must* say yes), his time for decision had ended and he had trusted to that niggling intuition and agreed to give it a shot.

The Untouchables was a monster success, and the long-running television series which followed firmly established the fame, fortune and artistic reputation of Robert Stack. It was the most important decision he had ever taken in his life. But was it fate, or coincidence, or something more, which let him know that the role of Elliot Ness was for him?

Donald Sutherland is another Hollywood actor who has found his career directed in this very strange fashion. In the late sixties he was a widely acclaimed rising star in the movie stables, but little known to the general public. A visit to a fortune-teller changed all that. He was directed towards a film which was to be made in a desert location and based around a villa. At the time no such movie was in the pipeline. Indeed, Sutherland was due to start work on an entirely different project. But the amount of detail offered on this big movie that would make his name was so incredible that he kept a look-out. Then fate intervened. The film which was due to take part in was unexpectedly cancelled. Up came the offer of another one, called *Joanna* – to be made in the deserts of Tangiers. All the other details which had been given to him matched, *except* for the villa, for the movie was set on a boat. However, on the cast's arrival for the shooting a last-minute change of plan by the producers took them from the boat to a much more suitable isolated house – the final missing piece in the strange jigsaw puzzle. The movie was a great success, and Donald Sutherland shared in its acclaim.

Sutherland was to find himself mixed up in an even more bizarre later event, when he made that delightfully spooky film *Don't Look Now* with Julie Christie.

Don't Look Now was based on a ghost story by Daphne du Maurier and contains some of the strangest sequences of dream and psychic phenomena ever portrayed on the screen. Sutherland and Christie played the parents of a young child, drowned in just a few inches of water in a pond outside their country home. The child comes back to haunt them, and the suspense of the movie and its eerie atmosphere derive from this.

But the eeriness did not end with the generous praise heaped onto their efforts in this fictional story. Six years later, in March 1979, Julie Christie drove herself to her own farmhouse in Wales with its own duckpond and small amount of water. A young couple were living in it with their son, not two years old. Julie found herself watching in horror as a tragic and amazing replay of the du Maurier novel was re-enacted. The body of the boy was found floating in the pond, and his mother waded into the water to bring him out. The scene in reality was virtually an exact reproduction of the one which pervades the movie, as Donald Sutherland wades in and Julie Christie gazes on.

How can such a coincidence occur? Is it a further coincidence that the actual theme of these events is psychic phenomena and a recurrent image of the drowning? It is almost as if that very thing has somehow repeated itself and translated from fiction into fact. One is left wondering where movies end and real life begins. But for the young family struck down by tragedy that seems rather inconsequential.

This whole subject is fascinating. I collect coincidences, both from my life and from these of others. I regard them as archetypal psychic phenomena, the one aspect of the paranormal which all of us touch from time to time. They patrol the outer limits of our rational universe and can, when understood, open up doorways to inner knowledge. For instance, in January and February 1983 I found myself involved in a strange sequence of events which are every bit as weird (but fortunately not as tragic) as those which Donald Sutherland and Julie Christie engaged in.

After deciding to do the second radio show in a thirty-week series which I had signed to do for Radio City, based on the subject of coincidences between twins, I found the theme repeating itself again and again. The day before my programme (without the radio station's knowledge of my subject), singer/songwriter Barbara Dickson appeared on air talking about her new play *Blood Brothers*, whose topic is coincidences between the lives of twins. In the post office, I was told that I had a twin who had just been in the shop. I left to find a Barbara Dickson song, appropriately titled 'January–February' being played in an adjacent store. And then I was invited to do a TV programme called *Tell the Truth* for Channel 4, in which I had to teach two girls to be my 'twins' so that a panel of celebrities could try to decide which one was really me and ask 'Would the real Jenny Randles please stand up?' One of the panellists was Willy Rushton, a bearded writer of comedy who is a near twin with Willy Russel, the bearded writer of comedy who penned the *Blood Brothers* musical play which started his merry-go-round on its inevitable path.

It does seem that our lives are sometimes intimately linked with what we may choose to call 'fate'. But do we have any control over it?

One of the other panellist I met on that Channel 4 show was

Claire Rayner, the famous agony-aunt. She has a remarkable ability which many would doubtless term psychic. For her it has the form of intense intuitions, which are invaluable for her work. She can sum up people or situations just by looking at them. And she often knows the right course of action by some sort of hidden sense. When the filming was over, Claire demonstrated this to me. The lounge at London Weekend Television, where the programme had been made, was crowded with people enjoying a buffet supper-party to wind down. Somewhere amongst us was one other real paranormal researcher, who had come as my guest. Instantly she could pick him out, with an uncanny astuteness which seemed almost like magic.

Of course, if you want to start quoting the laws of chance and reduce these human experiences to a pile of meaningless figures, you are quite at liberty to do so. Many scientists love that, hoping and even believing that arithmetic juggling will somehow wish away the problem. But to do this loses all sense of what it means to be alive in a world which we barely comprehend. It is like using your video recorder just to tell the time. The digital clock it usually has will certainly allow this, so one could persuade oneself that this must be its true purpose. Why press all the buttons or insert a tape, or do anything to learn the real function of this technological marvel? The answer is that you do not have to, if you do not wish. But look at what you are missing if you decline.

It is not simply Italian kings, Scottish folk-singers, playwrights and authors who find themselves in tune with the universe in this peculiar way. It is a common factor in scientific discovery. For example, in 1846, when the planet Neptune was found, two astronomers, John Adams in Britain and Urbain Leverrier in France, independently and simultaneously predicted where it should be. They did so based upon some dubious calculations and questionable maths. In fact, nobody is really quite sure just how one of them (let alone both at once) succeeded in obtaining the correct answer by asking most of the wrong questions. But no matter, because they did. Then John Galle in Berlin pointed his telescope exactly where the calculations told him to, and there was Neptune.

What seems to have happened is that the time became ripe for the discovery of this new planet. So Adams and Leverrier, as two minds in tune with one another and somehow in tune with the intangible laws of reality conspiring to allow this 'discovery', both responded to the influences around them. It is certainly quite fascinating that the astrological symbolism deduced for Neptune (and not an invention after the facts I hasten to add) contains the motifs: mystical, illusionary, hidden, obscure and psychic. The clouds of confusion surrounding the discovery, and the controversy over who should be granted the actual honour, plus the psychic rather than logical way in which it was made, all seem remarkably apt. As astrologers smile with delight, the material scientist shrugs and calls it a coincidence.

This is by no means the only occasion on which synchronicity has been involved in scientific discoveries. It often helps for the mind to slip out of 'normal reality mode' into what we might call 'synchronistic reality mode'. Daydreaming or ordinary dreams seem to be one way of affording this switch.

The chemist Friedrich von Kekulé could not work out how benzene atoms locked together. But after months of struggle he dozed in front of a fire and began to visualize snakes curling round and biting their own tails. His mind had slipped into srm (synchronistic reality mode) and tuned into the answer. It had then portrayed it to him by way of vivid imagery. The needle for the sewing-machine was invented in a similar way. And Leonardo da Vinci used to dream up his inventions. Indeed, he was frequently so far ahead of his time in this way that there was no practical method of implementing his schemes. Yet his diving costumes, submarines and helicopters have survived on paper.

In 1935 a young man lay in some meadows in Cambridge and, in a vision of the future whilst he entered srm briefly, visualized the world's first real computer. During the war this man, a mathematical genius called Alan Turing, invented just this and then went on to Manchester University to work on the first practical model. Unfortunately, soon after, at the young age of forty-two he died, when he ate a poisoned apple. Three weeks before, he had emerged ashen-faced and tight-lipped from the booth of a fortune-teller on Blackpool promenade. Nobody knows why.

Artistic people often seem to find it easier to make this switch in reality mode. Perhaps this is because they spend much of their waking life away from the normal mode. Certainly quite a few classical pieces of literature have their origins in dreams or visions or other examples of srm. We have seen how Robert Louis

Stevenson did this. In fact he often dreamt his stories as complete adventures. He claimed that his books 'wrote themselves'. Enid Blyton related how she wrote her captivating children's tales by simply relaxing in a chair, letting Noddy or Big Ears appear in front of her in a daydream, and then get on with acting out their story. She would sit like a detached observer, and later transcribe what she had witnessed as if she had just returned from the theatre. In a sense she was having controlled hallucinations brought to her, care of synchronistic reality.

Many successful and famous people have said that they put down their achievements to a 'little voice', by which they mean a form of intuition. More likely they are able (possibly without realizing it) to shift gears from normal reality into srm.

What is the difference between these two modes? In normal reality the mind perceives the world as we generally think of it. We can see the past and the present, but the future is yet to be. Nothing occurs unless some event or process causes it to occur. And the mind is just a passer-by, drifting through events it cannot control.

Synchronistic reality blurs time so that all levels are perceivable at once. Cause and effect become less reliable and may even break down altogether. And the mind is much more than a passer-by. It certainly does observe (with much wider horizons) but it can also influence events. Scientist Rex Stanford has a clumsy term 'Psi-Mediated Instrumental Response' for what is actually a simple idea. The mind, perceiving a situation that will benefit the individual, subconsciously manipulates either his actions or the actions of others, or both, and so manœuvres the person into circumstances which allow him to gain benefit. To the individual this might appear to be coincidence, or following one's nose. In truth it is neither. It is the most basic illustration of the ability we all possess, in srm, to facilitate the paranormal. Disliking cumbersome terms, I call these things 'prescripts'. The unconscious mind scripts the events in advance, and we, like actors, follow them along to undergo the 'coincidence'.

Real actor, and film star, Anthony Hopkins offers a nice example of this. He had signed to play a lead role in the movie of the novel *The Girl from Petrovka* but he could not find a copy of the book to read up on it. Finally he found himself at Leicester Square tube station, where he noticed a copy of a book literally discarded on a platform seat. It was of course the precise title he was after, and he was so pleased he did not even mind the curious notes written in the margin. Hopkins went abroad to make the movie and for the first time met George Feifer, author of the story. Feifer bemoaned the fact that he had lost a precious personal copy of his own book which he had annotated. He had lent it to a friend who had mislaid it whilst in London. The book was the same one which Anthony Hopkins had found by 'chance'.

Probably Feifer's unconscious mind had prescripted events to lead Hopkins to the right place at the right time. It is even possible that it worked in concert with Feifer's mind, longing for the return of his book. Both men were at the time linked together, although strangers hundreds of miles apart, by virtue of the forthcoming movie.

Another movie star, the diminutive American Red Buttons, offers another simple story to illustrate this principle. He was on a plane bound for New York and burying himself in a book, hoping that the passenger in the next seat would not recognize him and engage him in conversation about his work, from which he was endeavouring to escape. Finally, over dinner, Red Buttons changed his mind, and the two men struck up a conversation. The passenger explained that he was bound for Paris to bid on a major contract for his construction firm. Upon parting Red seized the opportunity of asking the man to call a friend of his in Paris and relay a message. The man agreed to this. When he reached Paris, the construction boss put through the call to Red's friend, a newspaper editor. They chatted amiably about the man's visit to France, and the construction worker mentioned that he felt he had little hope of winning the contract because a rival French company was likely to make a stronger offer. The editor then asked if the man would like to meet the head of his French rivals, the editor's own father-in-law! The meeting occurred, and it was found that both the American and French companies had things to gain by joining forces. This they did and together secured the contract.

Here you see how prescripting on a very simple matter led to a chain of circumstance which ultimately proved beneficial to a number of people. This is how true synchronicity can work.

It seems that wishes can come true. But we ourselves *make* them come true, with a little help from the deeper levels of our mind whilst in srm. If you are an artist, an actor, a scientist or just a human being, it might be worth remembering. We can prescript tomorrow out of today.

3. Curses!

'Reality is created by the law of habit' – Dr Rupert Sheldrake (biologist).

We have a family curse. I first met it when I was very young and of course never took it seriously. Nobody seems to know its origin, simply that it has existed throughout the past century and has constantly been vindicated. All close members of my mother's family are supposed to be doomed to die on a Tuesday.

Why a Tuesday we do not know – frankly it sounds quite absurd, but when my aunt died on a Tuesday the image of the curse was reinforced upon my young mind, and I have to admit that, in the two decades since, all the relevant deaths (four or five of them) have occurred on our death day. This includes my grandmother (in 1971) and grandfather (in 1975), both in my immediate presence at our home. On both occasions I vividly recall their sudden recovery on the Monday, with initial sighs of relief at this positive sign. But then a slow realization dawned. There does seem to be a temporary remission at the last moment, like a psychic calm before the storm of death. And of course I noted with horrible resignation the unalterable calendar as Monday ebbed to a close. Nobody referred to the curse until it was all over and somebody said with a murmur, 'Tuesday again.'

This is an eerie sensation, and I have no logic to explain it. Sometimes we think it is all an illusion. We are just ignoring non-Tuesday deaths. Or perhaps it is mere chance. And then there is the morbid temptation to wonder if, by believing in the curse (however half-heartedly), we somehow fuel its voracious appetite. Are we like aborigines willing ourselves to death through the power of autosuggestion?

I am not a superstitious person, but the effect of this little mystery always simmers beneath the surface of my life, and once or twice I have caught myself as worried about the day of the week as any other factor if illness strikes. I must sheepishly admit that in November 1983 I even rebooked a transatlantic flight when a computer error had me travelling on a Tuesday, even though this would have otherwise been acceptable. You may smile at such weak-willed behaviour, but if you do smile, it is clear that you have never had to face a curse.

This Tuesday syndrome is really a jinx rather than a curse. The latter presupposes some conscious act having decreed certain things not to be done, whilst the former has no obvious starting point. But for present purposes we might as well regard them as identical and stick to the terminology 'curse'.

Probably the most infamous is the one surrounding the opening the tomb of the Egyptian boy-king Tutankhamen. There is a curse long associated with Egyptian tombs, and this tomb, containing fabulous golden treasures, challenges any man who risks its desecration. He had to be very brave (or very foolish) to do so. Archaeologist Lord Carnarvon took his team to Egypt fully recognizing this fact, and he was even warned by the psychic Cheiro three months before he was ready to open the inner tomb. Later a palmist is said to have further advised against this action. But fate led Carnarvon blindly onwards, and he entered the tomb in the worst possible mood, challenging the curse with frivolity. (This seems to be the last thing one should do. Curses must always be given due respect.) Arthur Weigall, one of the excavators, told Carnarvon that if he behaved in this way he would not last six weeks. In fact, he survived seven before he fell to an infection following a mosquito bite. But this was just the early days of the curse. As the years went by, the number of fatalities grew. Weigall himself became victim number 21. And within seven years all but one of the excavators had died (many under curious or unusual circumstances).

Archaeologists obviously deny the curse. They claim it is either coincidence or a hoax invented by the tomb-robbers to keep unwanted visitors at bay. However, one or two people who have dismissed it in these terms have paid for their comments with an early death.

Oddly it seems that curses can extend to visual dramatizations. A TV movie, *The Curse of King Tut*, was made on location in 1979 but on the first day of shooting star Ian McShane crashed a vintage car being used in the scene and broke his leg in ten places. They had quite a task finding an actor to replace him! McShane said that the car seemed to be pulled towards a ravine by an outside power, and he had to leap from the vehicle seconds before it plummeted to destruction. In 1983 the TV company put in a massive insurance claim to Lloyd's for the delay, which they said had been caused by 'mysterious circumstances'. Lloyd's tried to argue that the car's brakes were faulty, so they could not be liable, but an undisclosed large sum was awarded by the judge, who clearly had more sympathy for the curse than the insurers.

Even so, it is terribly easy to view as part of the curse anything slightly unfortunate which takes place in connection with the matter. Once such a decision is subconsciously adopted, it all seems to fit like magic. When I decided to talk about the curse on my Radio City series in 1983, I suffered myself. Before each show I used to record a 'trailer' to promote the spot in the coming week, and the one about King Tut was easily the most problematic. Something went wrong again and again, and we had to re-do it several times.

Making movies about the paranormal does not seem like a particularly wise thing to do at the best of times. It is as if the creative process and intense concentration unleash psychic powers within the actors. The film *The Omen* is typical. Star Gregory Peck and author David Saltzer were both in planes struck by lightning (a rather appropriate retribution considering the demonic nature of the movie). The director was hit by a car and was then narrowly missed by a lightning strike, and the special effects man was in a horrific crash whilst driving in Holland. He survived, and actually regained consciousness staring at a sign for the town of Ommen.

Even stranger, though, were the events which surrounded the daring 1969 plan by Granada TV to film a series based on Alan Garner's macabre novel of possession and horror, *The Owl Service*.

Garner is a mysterious character who lives in a trailer-like home in a field in Cheshire. He has acquired a reputation as a sort of warlock, although he himself would deny that he is one. Yet he steeps himself in ancient legends, and his many novels based on them (such as *Red Shift*, about a time-slip, and *The Weirdstone of Brisingamen*, about the magic of one of Britain's most haunted places, Alderley Edge) have won the admiration of both children and adults. A dominating theme of his work is that time does not flow like a river, from past to future, but that one emotionally loaded experience can repeat throughout history in different guises, each interpreting the original event in a present-day manner. How this links in with the nature of a curse should be easy to see.

Peter Plummer, the producer of the TV series, has related the astonishing story of the writing of the novel and its almost immediate filming. It is so full of stupefying coincidence that the reader must consult his own words in the book, *I've Seen a Ghost*, in order to gain an adequate understanding.

Essentially Garner's story revolves around an ancient Welsh legend of a fatal love triangle, involving a fairy woman formed out of flowers to marry a warrior, who is doomed not to wed a human. After tragedy and murder, the flower-woman is turned into an owl. Garner wrote his story around this legend at a house he stumbled upon by accident which eerily matched the location in the tale. Then a set of Welsh plates came into his possession, and they were woven into his novel, for they bear a motif which, if looked at one way, resembles a bunch of flowers, and in another an evil owl. This appearance is obvious, I stress, and is certainly an intention on the part of whoever designed the plates (one must assume after the very same legend which Garner was now modernizing).

The making of the serial for TV was littered with owl situations. Every time fate took the crew to a particular location, something involving an owl would turn up there – a hidden door-knocker, an ornament banging shutters at midnight, or a live owl rescued from a bird attack which had taken up refuge in the room they were then using as the focal point of the programme! Such amazing things merely scratch the surface of the mysteries surrounding the series. The book, film serial, legend and real life all seemed to fuse in some incredible sense, just as Alan Garner's theories and writings suggest that they might.

Granada TV also features in the newest curse to associate itself with a series on the small screen – indeed, probably the most famous series British television has ever produced: the soap opera of life in an ordinary Lancashire town, *Coronation Street*. 'The Street' has been transmitted twice a week for over two decades and has been seen in most countries of the world. Generally it has ambled along quite happily, with occasional changes in characters and with mild traumas, but with a continuing group of actors playing out the scenes scripted for them in the never-ending saga. But then in 1983 things began to go dreadfully wrong.

At first it was innocent enough, although certainly poignant. The loss of Violet Carson (who played the Street's most famous old lady, 'Ena Sharples') and the later death of Jack Haworth (who played old soldier 'Albert Tatlock') were sad blows, but hardly unexpected in view of the ages of these originals from the show. Even the resignation, due to serious ill health, of another regular, pub-owner 'Annie Walker' (played by actress Doris Speed), might be regarded as just coincidence. The series could hardly afford to lose these three in such a short time-span, but the production team insisted it should fight on regardless. Another regular, Peter Adamson, who played builder 'Len Fairclough', brought disaster upon himself when he launched into an inexplicable tirade of criticism against his fellow actors in 'exposé' articles for a national paper. He was fired and 'killed off'. Soon after, one of the last surviving originals from the series, 'Elsie Tanner' (alias actress Pat Phoenix) walked out of the show and could not be persuaded to return. All of this would have been more than enough for any one year in the life of a TV soap, but what was already becoming rumoured as a curse was far from spent. Barbara Knox (who plays shop-owner 'Rita Fairclough') was struck down by a mystery virus and almost died. The very popular character bin-man 'Eddie Yates' (played by Geoffrey Hughes) decided to quit and go onto the stage. It was all most curious.

I recall one day, just before the curse rumours began to establish themselves, when I was at the Granada studios to take part in a programme about precognition. So much had happened to the series so quickly that most of its fans were just stunned. Before the programme about prediction we talked to the presenter about items to raise, and one lady announced that she had seen *Coronation Street* in a recent vision. There was soon going to be death of one of the principal characters, she told us all.

At the time most of the events connected with the series had not involved actual deaths, and Granada TV hardly surprisingly decided against using the woman's vision in the programme we were about to transmit. However, the next day actor Peter Dudley (who played the popular character Bert Tilsley') died, following what was described as some kind of 'breakdown'.

The tragic pattern continued into 1984 but showed signs of petering out. There were lawsuits, personal disasters and illnesses to the characters and Bernard Youens (the actor upon whom many commentators said the fate of the series now rested) died unexpectedly after an illness which had earlier cost him his leg.

About the only original, or long-standing, character now left (as I write) is William Roache (who plays journalist 'Ken Barlow'), and even he tragically lost his young child through illness in late 1984. Bill's explorations of the paranormal had long been known to me. He took a course to develop his astrological knowledge at the same time as I was studying the subject. Later he began to read a UFO magazine I edited and even attended a lecture on the subject which I helped to organize in Manchester. From these beginnings he went on to probe other areas of the psychic world and became interested in reincarnation and secret powers of the mind. By September 1984 he was giving public lectures on these phenomena and explained that it was tempting to ask the ·producers to allow some of his beliefs to filter through into his character. Although he said he had decided not to do so, 'Ken Barlow' did get involved in discussing both astrology and UFOs during 1984 episodes of the series.

Such a remarkable series of catastrophes, virtually decimating the original cast, all within so short a space of time, does appear to defy chance. The run of disaster seems at least the equal of that attributed to the Tutankhamen affair, or the *Owl Service* episode. Since both that serial and *Coronation Street* belonged to Granada TV, it is understandable that speculation should centre on their studios at Quay Street, beside the River Irwell in Manchester. I know these studios well, as a tall, square building with a rising transmission tower which reaches for the sky like a technological cathedral. It is one of Manchester's most obvious landmarks. Aside from quite a few TV programmes I have been involved with from there, for some years from 1975 onwards I used to attend regular meetings of a small band of researchers in one of the building's planning rooms. I recall that there was much talk of a ghost said to stalk the lower corridors, where the river edge passes closely and an old jail was reputed to have been. Also one member did enter what seems to have been a sort of a trance, turning white and with a reduced pulse in front of several witnesses. I would stress, though, that we were not there either to provoke or to research psychic phenomena (but rather UFO sightings from the north-west), and so the above information may well be unrelated.

Pat Phoenix seems to have known about strange 'feelings' in the area, however. And she took them a little further. She related the problems of the show to the temporary move to adjacent stables, converted into rehearsal rooms. 'I am convinced there must have been ley-lines there,' she added. William Roache, as you might expect, went along with this. He claims to have detected them. 'I suddenly felt this tremendous energy coursing through me,' he said. But he believes he was able to use it positively, to assert his character with the scriptwriters (and he did graduate during the time of the curse from a weak social worker to a crusading newspaper editor!) Others, Bill Roache insists, felt the same energy, but the power worked against them. Just like electricity, either it can shock you and leave you a burnt-out wreck, or it can be transformed into dynamism to power your way through life. In itself it is neutral, but it can be used for good or evil according to the medium through which it passes. We shall return to this idea later.

Just what are ley-lines (or leys, as the purists insist, since a ley *is* a straight *line*)? They are supposed lines of invisible force which cross the earth in a sort of network and are both demarked and focused into action by ancient structures at intersect points. Such markers might be stone circles or earthworks or churches constructed on even older religious sites. Even place-names ending in 'ley' (such as Alderley Edge) are said to be significant. The lines are thought to be natural products of the earth's 'biosphere', but sensed more acutely by ancient man as he was more 'in tune' with nature. This is why he located his holy places along their lengths. To the scientist they do not exist, of course – although a few are now having doubts about this assertion. Evidence does show that some kind of power is contained within stone circles, and a unique research project (called 'Dragon'), involving scientists, archaeologists and psychics, has compiled sufficient data to offer at least a tentative case for the reality of 'leys'.

If there is a ley focal point beneath part of the Granada studios and this can affect the minds of those who spend a lot of time there, now that the show has moved to its permanent accommodation it may well be that the problems are finally over. Certainly Granada TV and the millions of fans of its soap opera desperately hope so.

But can 'leys' be the true explanation for all curses? Surely not. Even if it were so on occasion, generally speaking the answer is unsatisfactory. However, if we develop the ideas which we first mooted in the last chapter, perhaps we can make progress towards some kind of over-all concept.

Sportsmen and women often speak of something they call 'the Peak Experience'. International golfer Tony Jacklin explains this well. He says that sometimes, when he is playing, he finds himself moving away from the everyday world. He leaves normal reality mode and enters synchronistic reality. Jacklin describes it as like a cocoon surrounding him, an invisible well of psychic power upon which he can draw. Once he taps this, he can perform way beyond his normal level. In football it is often said that two players can strike up an almost telepathic understanding with one another. Kevin Keegan and Terry McDermott, when playing for both Liverpool and Newcastle United, discovered this sort of principle. Often they would know instinctively where the other was going to be, so they could feed the ball through or receive it. There are those who say this contributed much to the great success of the two teams whilst they played.

The biologist Dr Rupert Sheldrake has designed experiments which set out to explain this sort of phenomenon. He argues that all living things possess a kind of 'life field'. Just as an invisible magnetic field is the originator of shapes and patterns formed by iron filings scattered over a card, so the field orientates our bodies and causes us to be what we are. It surrounds us, just like Jacklin's cocoon, and is the home of the mind and the various psychic phenomena to which it would seem to relate. How does this explain the telepathic understanding between footballers? Because one life field can interact with another even when there is no obvious, visible link. Just as two icebergs might rise above the surface of the sea and look to be well separated, yet down below the waters, where the bases of ice spread out, they touch one another, so in terms of these life fields each of us can share thoughts, feelings and experiences with someone else who maybe physically separate but psychically close.

But Sheldrake argues further. At the level of the life fields, or 'Species Field' (which is merely a term for the joining together of the various fields from any one species – e.g. all humans), information is transferable not only across space but also across time. Remember that, in synchronistic reality mode, past, present and future all seem to intertwine, and there is no clear dividing line between fact and fiction, or today and tomorrow.

American baseball star Roberto Clemente died in a plane crash on 31 December 1972, but his team mate Manny Sanguillen escaped by a miracle that was probably engineered by his life field detecting information essentially from the future (or what we would *call* the future in normal reality mode). Manny was originally due to fly on the 30th but he then learnt that the flight was delayed until the next day. When he came to drive to the airport twenty-four hours later, he could not find his car keys. After his searching everywhere, they eventually turned up in a very out-of-the-way location where he feels certain he did *not* put them. Now it was too late to get to the aircraft, which left on its death flight without him.

Somehow his mind had been aware of the coming events at the life-field level and had translated this information into actions (seeking out the keys fruitlessly, and so forth). It was an elaborate plan to hinder him sufficiently to prevent his reaching the airport on time. Sometimes this might manifest much more obviously as a 'bad feeling' or a 'premonition'. On other occasions, it seems, this vague scrambling of normal bodily functions is all that our deeper levels of awareness are able to achieve.

Sheldrake believes that all our behaviour, as well as our physical form, is created by the invisible life fields which surround us. He calls the principle by the fancy name of 'morphic resonance' (which just means that forms are created by layering one field on top of another, and so on, until an average or 'norm' is created). When an average, or norm, results from life fields which direct human behaviour, this produces a path which our lives tend to follow, like raindrops falling down a slanting roof gradually eating out a channel in that roof, which then acts as a focus for all future drops of water falling on there. Whenever the trend is a nasty one, we may end up with a curse.

As Kevin Keegan's successful manipulation of the life-field energies gave his football club Liverpool success, so their great rivals from the same city, Everton, were faced with bigger and bigger disasters. As they lost games, could not score goals and tumbled down the league tables, so they decided to sign on a new player – a woman! She was not to take part in the conventional sense of the word; instead, being a well-known local psychic, she was to concentrate her life-field energies on Everton FC and try to bring them back to winning ways. Amazingly, it worked. The reinforcing of this positive image within the species field began to filter through. Just like a curse, but this time working in a helpful not destructive manner, 'Everton will win' became a norm. And being a norm it began to happen. As I write, at the end of 1984, Everton FC have won the FA Cup (in the season after this psychic assistance was seconded) and stand at the head of the First Division championship race, a position their fans never dreamt possible less than two years before!

The Chicago Cubs, an American baseball team, have had similar ups and downs due to the intervention of the curse of a goat! Innkeeper 'Billy Goat' Sianis used to attend matches with a pet goat as a mascot, but when he took it to the World Series finals in 1945 and was thrown off the ground, he imposed the curse and said the team would never win again. Since then they have had a disastrous run, but came closest to success in 1973 when Sianis temporarily returned with a new goat. But he was later banned once more, when it seemed as if the curse was finally broken. Soon the team plummeted down the table, and they are still trying to decide whether they should swallow their pride and put up with a goat in their ranks, or else run the risk of never winning anything again. We might say, in terms of Sheldrake's theory, that the goat and attendant failure became a behaviour norm in the species field, acted out through the life fields of all their players (causing them to play worse than they otherwise would). The result is what looks like a curse.

Doubtless the many sporting jinxes and curses have similar origins. Sport instils great passions into players and fans, and it does seem to be the emotions which are most in touch with these life fields. If you stir them up, you can apparently make life very hard indeed. The only way to 'exorcise' a curse seems to be to create an equally powerful belief that it does *not* work in the minds of those it operates through because they believe that it does.

'Belief' is the key word here. It would seem that what we choose to believe in hard enough can actually come to pass in the real world. What we do at the level of our life field works itself out as good or bad events. All those who say that positive thinking can make miracles happen do appear to know what they are talking about.

Does this explain all kinds of curse? It seems unlikely. Probably this effect, which as suggested is akin to a primitive aborigine willing himself to die because he believes a witch doctor has ordained that he must, can account for some of the long-range historical phenomena. Another option is proposed by the case of King Casimir's tomb, opened in 1973 on the orders of then Cardinal Karol Wojtyla, now Pope John Paul II, to be inspected by a team of scientists. One by one the scientists and the historians who worked on the project began to die! Naturally a curse, activated by the desecration of the grave, was held to blame. However, after much diligent research Professor Smyk, a microbiologist, found the real culprit. A tiny virulent microbe released by the opening of the five-hundred-year-old tomb had entered the bloodstream of those closely associated with the study. All those with pre-existent medical problems found these aggravated, and many of them died.

That curse had a very real existence and a very real explanation, and we might be tempted to think this is true of many cases where objects are involved, but there are times when this stretches things to the very limit.

Teenage idol, film star and cult hero James Dean died in 1955, when his car was wrecked. The bizarre events which came to befall the car are now as much a legend as Dean himself. First the car's engine fell from its perch at the garage to which it had been taken. It broke both legs of the mechanic working on it. When put it a racing car, it failed, and the driver was again killed. In the same race another driver died. His car had taken the drive-shaft from Dean's cursed vehicle. Later the car's remains continued to leave a trail of disaster., including a huge fire. The curse finally ended in 1959, when the car was standing alone on display and literally just fell to pieces!

4. Memories of Another Life

'What past-life regression is hardly matters, what counts is that I use it to cure people' – Joe Keeton (hypnotherapist).

One of my favourite movies stars Barbara Streisand and is based on the Broadway play *On a clear day you can see forever*. On a recent visit to the USA I sat up all night to watch it for about the fifth time. The hour enhanced what to me is a truly magical spell which it casts.

The plot has Streisand being hypnotized to stop her smoking; she proves such a good trance subject that she spontaneously slips into recollections of past lives. In each of these she and the hypnotist have shared romantic liaisons. I suppose this appeals because the subject of reincarnation does. For many who have studied the prospect that we each live many lives, it seems to strike a hidden chord and somehow *appears* to be right. One can never explain how or why. Of course, there is a vast difference between intuitively sensing the 'rightness' of something and being able to prove it, even if that something does offer explanations for puzzling things such as why children can be born with gross disabilities or why, as they say, 'the good die young'. Viewing life as a continuing process, with our current run of three score years and ten little more than today's lesson in the long school calendar, brings to me an instant sense of recognition, almost a mystical illumination. It *feels* like a great, cosmic truth. That does not necessarily count for anything, but I would never bank on it.

Perhaps it is only the fact that it offers us all a defence against our greatest fear – death. That would probably be as good an answer as any to most scientists.

The Streisand movie is a light-hearted romp but firmly rooted in possible reality. Under regression hypnosis *thousands* of people have now recalled 'past lives' (for, as in the movie, one person can often be led to describe several at various points back through time). Of course, this in itself does not prove that reincarnation is fact (there could be other explanations) but it does offer a surprisingly consistent set of experiences which demand some sort of answer. Unfortunately, yet again, science prefers to believe that the problem does not exist.

Henry Mancini, the famous musician and composer, is one of the thousands to be regressed. This happened shortly after the end of World War II, when he was on leave in France. He was young and willing to try what was suggested to him as an interesting experiment after meeting a hypnotist socially. Mancini slipped easily into trance, but when he was encouraged to recall previous lives, he at first found nothing happening. Then random thoughts began to enter his head, and he had 'impressions' – one of being a soldier years ago, another of living as the classical composer Verdi. As he admitted, it was quite impossible to tell whether such thoughts had really welled up from his subconscious memory or if they were merely examples of an active imagination. Certainly he was less than convinced by them, and it is true that both sound exactly like the sort of thing a man dreaming of becoming a geat composer having just emerged from a bitter war *would* imagine.

Now that we understand the curious state of consciousness called hypnosis a little better, it would seem that imagination is the best candidate in Mancini's case. Under hypnosis the ego (the controlling sense of 'I') is weakened, and this allows one to be subtly directed by implied suggestions from the hypnotist. It also enhances imagination and role-playing, although it is true that it facilitates memory too. One is always forced to choose between all these options (or possibly a mixture of several) when assessing the origin of any data retrieved via hypnosis.

However, after those first images, Mancini's memory *did* flood out. He could see himself amidst a hot desert landscape, where he was a simple labourer working very hard. A great monument, possibly the Sphinx itself, was in the process of being built. The hypnotist asked Mancini to write down his views on the giant structure and (still in a trance) he did so. The writing was in pictogram form, not unlike hieroglyphs. When he was brought round, he could not believe he had written it. It looked like nonsense to everyone present. Some months later, after his return home, he was told by his brother in France that the writing had been taken by the hypnotist to the local museum. Here it had been recognized as some form of Egyptian, but nobody could translate it. Whether this was because it had been obscure labourer's 'slang', or because it was pseudo-Egyptian made up by the subconscious mind of the composer, is the big question that remains without answer. As I said, under hypnosis the mind is perfectly capable of *both* super memory and super-creative ability. Which of these produced the hieroglyphs?

To most who are unacquainted with past-life studies, it might well be anticipated that many of the accounts would be memories of life as a famous person (e.g. Mancini's recall of his incarnation as Verdi). In fact the complete opposite is true. In the hypnotic experiments I have personally witnessed, the three people involved remembered fairly ordinary lives: as a Sussex farmer, a rather sickly bedridden child and a poor 'lady of the streets'. Hardly the stuff of romantic fantasies! This mundane nature of past lives is the rule. It is very much an exception to profess to have been a celebrity of the past.

One person who did just this was a Lancashire housewife, Edna Greenan. In her broad accent she is able to acquire the character of Nell Gwynn, the young girl who rose from street urchin to famous actress and then became mistress (and illegitimate-child bearer) of King Charles II. Eighty hours of tape record sessions in which Edna 'becomes' Nell. She can flash about from one age to the next and always act in character and relevant to the times. Even if she were well read on Nell Gwynn so as to know most of the facts, this instant time-switch would still be an amazing phenomenon – of extreme psychological (not to say human) interest. Think of its application to acting, entertainment and historical research if it could be harnessed!

Yet this is typical of genuine regression experiments. If the solution does turn out to be some form of dramatization by our subconscious minds, it shows that we all possess inside us such remarkable acting talent that the real Nell Gwynn would appear incompetent. Yet almost nobody who is regressed claims acting talent, at least in their everyday lives. Even though we accept that hypnosis can stimulate this, is that sufficient to explain the marvels that we see?

Here is a typical passage where Nell Gwynn (alias Edna) is trying to sell fish as a young child on the streets:

'Do you want fresh herrings, lady?' she cries. 'Yes . . . they are fresh. I've just chopped the bleedin' head off that one.'

And again, when she is dying in her bed, she says: 'Do you think it's time?'

'Time for what?' hypnotist Joe Keeton requests.

'Time I spoke th'epilogue now.'

Such things come out spontaneously and repeatedly, with great realism. There is no stuttering or pause. And the same applies if they are asked about major historical facts or minor incidents in their lives. If an old priest is asked to talk in Latin, he does so. If someone is asked their age after being previously regressed to a given year, there is no hesitation and the age is correctly offered.

But at times decidedly false or imaginative information gets offered just as freely. This puzzling fact is an aspect of the basic hypnosis phenomenon and is not peculiar to past-life study. A person taken back to his schooldays will have a much enhanced recall and visualize himself as he was in those days. Remarkable (but demonstrably accurate) data can be extracted even when totally unknown to his conscious mind. And this will be coupled with a sort of acting (in which he will simulate his writing at the time, for instance). To this will be added false information, which he either guesses or invents without realizing it. Do not forget that even one century ago there was no television or radio and far fewer newspapers. Even major facts were relayed mostly by gossip, and (as would be obvious to anybody who listens to chatter on a street corner today) this could easily produce gross misconceptions, especially in the past-life stories of ordinary folk.

It is perfectly possible that in a past-life memory all of these factors are involved, and so it is difficult to know in any one instance what percentage of the information used to construct the life is *real* memory, and what percentage guesswork or invention. Of course, you may be inclined to believe that the percentage of real memory is always nil in past-life cases, on the grounds that there are no past lives and so the phenomenon is impossible. In that case it must all be guesswork or invention. But there are some arguments against this, and it can be shown in regression to previous times in *this* life that real memory of a remarkable kind can be accessed. So there is no inherent reason why past-life testimony cannot contain factual data.

Of course, when we face the prospect of just chancing upon the person in this life who was Nell Gwynn in another, it looks rather convenient, but there are few such instances and thousands of regressions. There are also quite a large number of people whom we might reasonably term 'famous' during the history of the world. So if one looks at it in this way, it is not that amazing that Edna Greenan should have come along.

Let us now turn to some famous people in this life and see what sort of memories they produce under hypnosis. That will serve to emphasize the point I have just made and show the difference between Mancini's 'life' as Verdi and his more concrete impressions of the Egyptian labourer. Fame and fortune in the twentieth century do *not* presuppose the same thing in a past-life memory.

Singer Vince Hill went under hypnosis at the hands of a London dentist, Leonard Wilder. In this experiment he recalled a very vivid life which unravelled, as he put it, 'like a film', in which he was a farmhand in an Essex village, born around 1649. He went on to marry a girl called Mary and have a son called James. He describes the L-shaped farmhouse he came to live in, the food he ate, clothes he wore, methods of farming, how Mary left him and how at the age of forty-seven he fell down the stairs and died. All very ordinary and banal. Vince was most impressed by all the little incidents, each of which he saw clearly but which mostly involved very trivial things. To him it all seemed very real. To us it just seems human.

Impressionist Faith Brown was hypnotized in the same manner. In her subconscious she is steeped with imagery caused by 'becoming' famous people all the time. If anyone should invent a famous past life, one might expect her to. Yet she just became Frances Jenkins, born in 1779, who had an affair with a married judge called Gerald. When Gerald went back to his wife and then died soon after, under slightly mysterious circumstances, this produced mental unbalance in Frances and accusations of murder against her. At the age of forty she describes being locked up in an asylum, pronounced insane and fed bread and water under miserable conditions.

Diane Solomon, an American singing star, was the third subject. Her memories were more detailed. She recalled no fewer than four lives. In one she saw herself as a young Greek girl tied to her sister and being whipped by Romans who had attacked and burnt her home. At an unspecified date she described a short life as Martha Grey, who lived in Mississippi and died in great pain from tuberculosis. 'It wasn't imagination. I really felt it – and it hurt,' she said of this. The last two lives are fairly uneventful but problematic for another reason. She becomes Jonathon Miller, born in 1763 as a pioneer settler of the West, moving out from Des Moines. His life concerns building up a farm, having a family, trading molasses with Indians and then dying (aged fifty-eight) in 1821, with some disease in his leg. However, she also gives details of a life as Katrina, a girl from Washington, with fairly wealthy parents. She talks of just simple things – dresses, parties, theatre trips and so on – but she adds that she died in 1870, having been born in 1817. If this is not an error, it produces a rather awkward four-year overlap with Jonathon Miller! What is more, a historian who assessed the cases for the newspaper who funded the project explained that Des Moines did not exist in the eighteenth century, and the pioneer's tale makes sense only if brought forward about half a century. This only compounds the difficulty. (All this assumes that our traditions are correct and that the Des Moines which Miller talks about is the same one the historian infers.)

However, such 'goofs' are a minor (but far from insignificant) feature of past-life regression, and the essential point these three experiments demonstrate is that the remembered lives are again of a routine level. If they are produced as imaginative constructions, dramatizing half-retrieved stories or fantasies, why are they not far more exciting or adventurous? One would especially imagine that 'show-biz' personalities would invent interesting lives. Also, why does the death of the person assume great importance? It is one of the things constantly described by the subject, although historical stories concentrate on the life (not death) of their characters.

Generally speaking, if a person is asked to 'home in' on a past life under hypnosis, one vivid scene will emerge. This is often the person's death or some trauma (e.g. Faith Brown locked away,

Diane Solomon being whipped by marauders). That would be what we might expect if there are *real* memories of the past hidden inside us. We would tend to go first for the emotional connections. After this it is mostly trivia which is recalled, which is exactly how we remember the past of this life.

The way in which these hypnosis experiments seem to duplicate real-life recall may be one of the most evidential facts in their favour.

We might well ask why past lives do not seem to be wish-fulfilment fantasies (rather like daydreams). Why do we not usually see ourselves rich and famous, or living on a desert island and so forth? Past-life recall is stocked with the usual grim legacy of human misery – indeed, often more so than today. This is important, as we have romantic illusions about the past while, in truth, life was often very harsh and cruel. There was illness, poverty and hardship, and nothing like the medical and social facilities we have today to combat them. Whilst historical fiction undersells these facts, regression hypnosis would appear to reveal the bare truth remarkably well.

Robert Reiff and Martin Scheerer are two scientists who studied hypnosis before it came to be widely used for past-life regression. In 1959 they wrote about 'age regression' to younger times in *this* life. They said that regression was facilitated if the person was asked to relive an emotional day. This supports such events being the easiest for spontaneous recall in past-life studies. Reiff and Scheerer determined three types of regression: (a) role-play fantasy (or a kind of acting); (b) reliving a real psychological state; (c) a mixture of both the above. In their view most age regression consisted of varying mixtures of (c), with different degrees of real data feeding role-play acting. Past-life regression may be very similar, but to demonstrate that real memory can emerge from age regression they experimented to show that subjects taken back to childhood develop IQs that are the same as in adult life but answer psychology tests as if they were children of the relevant age. One man who suffered from an abnormal brain pattern after the age of eighteen lost this when regressed to childhood, provided he was told to be younger than the age at which the abnormality began.

Reiff and Scheerer also conducted experiments where they regressed people to the ages of four, seven and ten and asked a control group to simulate behaviour at these ages. Typical results showed that, if subjects played in mud and were then suddenly handed a lollipop, all would suck it, but the control group tended to wipe the mud off their hands first, while those regressed just went straight for the sweet! There were many similar illustrations that regression is somehow genuine reliving. If subjects were asked to name the day of the week as they relived a past birthday, they could do so. Should they be using super mental arithmetic to achieve this, rather than direct access to memory data, it should be no less easy to work out this information for the ages of ten, seven or four. In fact the accuracy decreased from 93 per cent (at ten), through 82 per cent (at seven) to 69 per cent (at the age of four). This certainly suggests a form of real memory. Young children would be less aware of the day of the week than older ones.

Many modern psychologists have made systematic studies of the possibility of reincarnation. Dr Helen Wambach has produced a massive set of statistics based on two thousand past lives she has collated. Every factor seems to demonstrate the validity of a real phenomenon. White people remembered being coloured and displayed no sign of inbred racial prejudice. The proportion of sexes, stations in life and lengths of life were all what one would historically expect.

Dr Edith Fiore has been particularly interested in the way in which phobias can be cured by the use of past-life therapy. She notices a connection between supposed violent death or tragedy in a past life and some form of phobia in this one. For instance, a patient paranoid about the colour red, who could not even touch it, under hypnosis 'recalled' a previous lifetime in which as a child she had witnessed her mother being stabbed to death in a terrible bloodbath. As Dr Fiore asks, if the memory of the past life is not real, why does the reliving of it through hypnosis usually cure the phobia? It is as if it acts like a safety valve letting off great gushes of psychic steam.

Comedian and entertainer Roy Hudd has a tale which he loves to tell that might just be in this category.

Hudd has a great passion for the old-time music-hall, a form of variety he feels very much attached to but which he is too young to have experienced. Often he presents television programmes on this theme, and he has even produced one 'special' about the great Victorian star Dan Leno. Leno was a comedian, much in Roy Hudd's mould, who burnt himself out both mentally and physically and died tragically young. He is widely considered one of the most brilliant performers which the last century produced.

Roy Hudd's great interest in Dan Leno has a curious starting point. It began with a long series of dreams about a house. He saw it inside and out and could recall many details. One vivid image concerned multiple pictures of himself, which later he came to realize was the effect of being surrounded by mirrors. The dreams started when Roy was a child and were very persistent throughout his young adult life. Although the emotions attached to them were never bad, the similarities with the phobias which Edith Fiore studies are fairly apparent. Many of these came to the patient in the form of recurring dreams.

One day Roy Hudd and his wife were invited to visit some friends in their new house in a part of London he had never seen. They searched around for the house and arrived at the road where they believed it to be. Instantly Roy recognized the surroundings. Indeed, he could direct his wife to the precise house long before they could see the number. They sat outside, staring at it, whilst the comedian, now decidedly serious, proceeded to give as much detail as he could remember from his dreams about what the house should look like inside. He was proved correct in virtually every detail. Even the mirrors fitted. The house had, you see, once been the home of Dan Leno. (There was a plaque on the wall put there by the council to announce this fact.) Leno had used a room filled with mirrors to practise in so he could observe his act as the audience would see it.

Once Roy Hudd realized this, the impact of his repetitive dreams was enormous. They had been so frequent and so vivid that he knew this was neither coincidence nor imagination. He *had* visited this same house again and again in his dreams, long before he had ever set eyes on it. But he had also viewed it in the way that it was when Leno owned it. This realization acted as the catharsis and released the emotional safety valve, just as hypnosis does with Fiore's patients. He never had the dreams again, but he was motivated strongly enough to research the life of Dan Leno and produce his TV special.

Just what is the explanation for this spooky story? Roy Hudd does not know. It has been mooted to him that perhaps Dan Leno chose him as a protégé and is watching over him from the 'other side'. The dreams were the first attempts at communication and a means of initiating the entertainer's interest in his unknown mentor. But Roy Hudd seems to have a sneaking attachment for the possibility that he might actually *be* Leno! In other words Roy Hudd *was* the Victorian comedian in a past life, and so the dreams were vestigial memories of his life and times in a bygone age.

Ridiculous as this might seem on the face of it, there are some things which act in its favour. The personal similarities between Hudd and Leno, for example. Is genius something which is carried over from one life to the next? Perhaps musical prodigies, if put under hypnosis, would recall a previous existence as a famous composer? Indeed the return of Verdi as Henry Mancini might on this basis not be as crazy as it seems!

Joe Keeton is one of the most prolific therapists who uses regression to past lives to cure people. He has regaled me with countless amazing stories. To him claims of regrowing parts of the human body and curing apparently incurable ailments are almost everyday events. (When he supposedly got rid of eye cancer from a famous surgeon, the surgeon is said to have considered giving up his work, because, in his words, he felt like a fraud.) Keeton insists that most past-life regressions are not genuine. He can always spot when a person is truly reliving a previous experience. The further back in time they go, the greater the difficulty in understanding them. Before the year 1400, he says, they speak in such an incomprehensible way that it is impossible to hold a conversation. As a 'baby' they just crawl about and slobber!

Most of the phenomena witnessed in the guise of past lives are, according to many researchers (including Keeton), due to cryptomnesia. This is a mental process whereby the mind retains literally everything it has ever had fed into it – every sentence spoken, image seen, book read, television programme viewed and so forth.

Our mental self is made up of a series of interlocking boxes, rather like the Russian dolls which slot into another one of slightly larger size. The conscious mind is the smallest doll, containing all our normal memories and emotions. This slots into the subconscious, which includes all of this plus root instincts and data we use but do not need regular access to (e.g. knowledge of how to ride a bicycle). At the deepest level is the unconscious mind, which contains both the things just described but also includes data of a cryptomnesiac kind. If we want to get hold of something, all experiences we have ever had lie there awaiting access. We may say that we have never read about a farmer in rural Essex or been told about the great Victorian entertainer Dan Leno, but that knowledge might well be there somewhere inside our unconscious.

It is at this level that the interlocking of minds occurs. The unconscious is probably the equivalent of the life field in most respects. When life fields of millions of people overlap, we have a species field, or, as Carl Jung called it, the 'Collective Unconscious'. Here he saw the basis of all myths and legends common from race to race across our planet. We might be separated physically by the great oceans or the width of continents, but on a mental level our unconscious minds merge. As we all belong to one species, wherever we come from on the earth, at this mythic plane we share a great deal. In terms of the collective unconscious, everything that any of us has ever experienced is potentially available. What price true reincarnation then?

A number of careful investigators, such as Ian Wilson, have already successfully traced many classic past-life cases back to vestigial memories that had been totally forgotten. In the conscious and subconscious minds they did not exist, but cryptomnesia under the special state of hypnosis made them available from out of the unconscious.

Of course, if there *is* a species field, as we have proposed, and this is independent of both space and time, as some of the cases we have been examining in other chapters suggest, a form of reincarnation might be possible *without* any of us having lived before. We might gain access to information direct from this gigantic pool of knowledge and build a fantasy around it. The belief that we were a long-dead person would be false, but the information about them might be true.

That this is feasible is best demonstrated by the fact that not all past-life memories come by way of hypnosis. Indeed, if Roy Hudd's case is one of reincarnation, it is true of that. Dr Ian Stevenson, a psychiatrist from Virginia State University, has travelled the world collecting cases of spontaneous memory, usually from young children. He found that on average they begin to speak of their previous lives at the age of three years one month and stop doing so (with no later recall) at five years four months. Strangely the child often claimed to be a former member of the same family he had been reborn into. He had often died suddenly whilst still young. In one-fifth of the cases the details offered were checkable and did prove correct.

One of the most amazing examples of this type of case is British. Stevenson has already professed his support for it, and even Ian Wilson agrees that, if it were to be proved genuine, it would be very hard to refute. But the problem is that it relies almost entirely on the word of the father (the only surviving parent), the two children involved (both now adults) having no real memories of it at all. That father has a strong predisposition to *believe* in reincarnation and had a conviction before the fact that the events which allegedly happened would indeed happen. Obviously his new ideas must have had an effect on his children, who would have no desire to rebel against their parents. But can this explain this strange case?

It centres on Hexham, Northumberland, when Joanne and Jacqueline Pollock (aged eleven and six) were tragically killed, along with a young friend, as a car driven by a woman intent on suicide accidentally smashed into them whilst they walked between their home and the local church on 5 May 1957. Their father, John Pollock, interpreted it as divine retribution for his belief in reincarnation. Praying for some sort of sign of forgiveness, he became convinced that his wife would shortly have twins and that they would be his dead daughters reborn. There was no history of twins in either family, and when his wife did indeed become pregnant, the doctors insisted that only one baby was in the womb. Nevertheless, on 4 October 1958 Florence Pollock did give birth to twins, Gillian and Jennifer. Jennifer was allegedly born with a thin scar on her forehead, identical to one Jacqueline had gained when she fell off her bicycle aged two, but this scar soon faded. Jennifer *does* still have a birthmark on her hip, in the same place as Jacqueline used to, but that is hardly overpowering evidence in view of the genetic ties.

When the twins were just four months old, the family moved to a new home thirty miles from Hexham. But when they were three, John decided to arrange a visit back to the old house to see if this would jog any memories in his daughters. It did. The girls allegedly recognized the house and even correctly named dolls which their predecessors had played with. Did John prompt them into this? Or could they have obtained such information through telepathy or even more normal means?

The most dramatic event which John Pollock claims came when the twins were playing outside and began to scream as a car engine started up. He says that when he reached them they were clutching one another, crying 'The car! The car! It's coming at us!' – all because the car was presenting to them the same angle as the one in 1957 must have presented itself to Joanna and Jacqueline in their final moments. By the time the girls were six they had forgotten all of this, which makes honest assessment of the case difficult. But this does fit the pattern which Ian Stevenson claims to have found.

For their book *Life Before Life* Peter and Mary Harrison collated many cases such as this. They too fit the pattern. For instance, they talk of four-year-old Nicola Peart, from Keighley, West Yorkshire, who had a vivid recollection of life as a boy who lived at Haworth (a village just a couple of miles away). She knew the family name (Benson), the name of her (his) dog (Muff) and lots of other detail. She spoke of being killed by a train and described doctors at the hospital asking how 'he' was but being unable to walk or talk. Kathleen Peart, Nicola's mother, decided to take her daughter to Haworth (where allegedly she had never been). Not only did Nicola direct her there and then onto her 'old home', which matched her previous descriptions very well, but when the parish registers were checked evidence was discovered that a boy named John Benson (born on 20 June 1875) might have been the former incarnation of little Nicola.

One major question which many of these child memory cases poses is why the two lives are geographically so close together. This and the family link already referred to are far more common than logic suggests they should be. Sceptics will doubtless point out that such facts make it easier for the child to absorb both local and family information.

Whatever the truth about reincarnation, it can at times take over a person's current life. The very poignant tale of the renowned playwright Ada F. Kay demonstrates this. (Ian Wilson has made a special study of her bizarre claims but has so far reached no final conclusion.) She alleges that before she began to write plays and books about Scottish history she started to experience very strong mental flashbacks of life as King James IV of Scotland. One of her first images, complete with pain and terror, was of her (his) death on the battlefield at Flodden when the English attacked in 1513. The amount of memory she claims about her life as the Scottish king is so astonishing that she has written a book that spans a quarter of a million words based on what she has seen. But more disturbing is the way her slow reawakening to her past 'existence' has destroyed her marriage and home life in the twentieth century.

Ada (now known as Ada Stewart) wears clothes that would be appropriate to the king but which look decidedly odd today. Her home in Edinburgh is littered with artefacts and memorabilia from the sixteenth century. She even claims a physical resemblance to the king. Her identification with the personality of the man from 4½ centuries ago is almost total and to the unprepared very eerie.

Not knowing Ada, or having seen her work and the obviously gifted mind that lies behind it, one may easily be tempted to chuckle or feel pity for this fifty-five-year-old woman. But that misses the point, and Ada does not seem to feel sorry for herself. Perhaps she ought to. As the law stands at this moment, she cannot claim the title or land to which her remarkable family tree might entitle her.

5. Public Figures and the Paranormal

'The existence of these machines is evident and I have
accepted them absolutely' – Lord Dowding, Air Chief
Marshal.

In May 1812 John Williams, a Cornish innkeeper, had a very
strange dream, which occurred three nights in succession. The
image seemed to be of the House of Commons and involved a
prominent politician being shot. John Williams had no idea who
this might be, living so far from London in an age when news
travelled only as fast as the quickest stagecoach. But when he told
a relative, who did frequent London, Williams was shocked to
discover that his description appeared to match Spencer
Perceval, then Prime Minister. Several days later the news
filtered through to Cornwall that Spencer Perceval *had* been
murdered in the lobby of the House of Commons, just as John
Williams had dreamt.

Was the dream a vision of the future (a premonition) or a
telepathic message relayed across space but not time by the dying
PM or the intending murderer? In such cases it is often very
difficult to decide. Indeed, sceptics will insist that it was just a
coincidence. Leaders of state are always liable to assassination
attempts. It is no big deal to think you have predicted one.
Nevertheless, as many other examples in this book will
demonstrate, the Williams/Perceval experience is one of a
sufficiently large body of evidence to suggest that, whatever the
truth, it is more interesting than chance or coincidence.

British prime ministers have been linked to the paranormal on other occasions, and a random skip through some of these reported events will be of interest.

The first example is one to which researchers in this area are all too accustomed. It is a fantastic tale, told as true by those who reported it, but with precious little else to support its veracity. It concerns a family (mother, father and their teenaged son) who moved into a rambling old house among the Welsh mountains. It was, so they were informed, the erstwhile home of a man who had been a prime minister during the past century. When an old man he had allegedly hanged himself in one of the bedrooms, although this story was not often talked about and hard facts are scarce.

With that sort of welcome to their new home it is hardly surprising that odd things allegedly started to happen almost right away. The sound of footsteps walking the hall was heard repeatedly, all the bedroom doors would open for no obvious reason, and at one point the figure of an old man with white beard and military uniform was seen walking along the landing and vanishing into an empty, windowless room whose door was locked. And then the wife began to have dreadful forebodings about the house, insisting that their 'ghost' (who was naturally assumed to be the former prime minister) was trying to warn them to leave. Following a terrible nightmare she finally announced that she had foreseen their sixteen-year-old son being knocked down and killed miles from home by a 'black coach or carriage'. Yet the family stayed in the house.

Two weeks later the father went to the bedside of Alan, their son, following his calls in the dead of night. Alan pointed to the wall behind his bed and asked what the strange circle of coloured lights might be. His father examined it, but it moved off. There were no mirrors to produce stray reflections, and only remote unlit fields outside. What it was they had no idea, and they claim not to be aware that such 'circles of light' are a common type of phenomenon, often reported in haunted bedrooms. The light having now gone, Alan inquired about the strange bearded man whom he had seen walking through the door before vanishing. His father told him that he was probably just dreaming. But Alan had been occupying the room where the tragedy had occurred.

The next day, some way from home, Alan was struck by a black saloon car on a country road. He was thrown fifty yards into a field, where he died. In his pocket was discovered a faded photograph of an old bearded man, who had once been a British prime minister. Nobody knew how it had got there.

One is tempted to say that if you believe that you will believe almost anything, and to me it resembles an attempt at inventing a horror story. But the family and the house both exist, and the case was reported to ASSAP, apparently in good faith.

On a much sounder footing is the fact that the first official statement ever offered about UFOs came from the future Prime Minister, but then First Lord of the Admiralty, Winston Churchill as long ago as 27 November 1912. It followed some weird events one month before at Sheerness, Kent, when a mysterious buzzing object passed overhead and villagers lit flares assuming some form of unidentified aircraft was due to land. Nothing did come down, and Churchill was forced to initiate a style which was to become popular much later when he insisted that, although the British government knew of the report, they had no explanation to offer – but there was nothing to worry about.

However, people did worry about encounters (of which the Sheerness event was but one) with what came to be known as the 'mystery airship'. Over the first few months of 1913 there was a whole spate of sightings, sometimes quite impressive. Popular belief was not, as you might expect, that little green men were invading 'Blighty', but rather that the ships were of German origin on a spying mission over Britain's shores as a prelude to an imminent landing. The tension leading up to World War I helps put this into context. However, it is extremely improbable that German airships did overfly Britain, and their performance over the years to come (when one presumes any craft would have been better than these 1913 prototypes) also supports that negative view. Many researchers think that panic created many misperceptions and over-imagination – more or less the same as sceptics argue today when 'mystery spaceships' are reported instead. But whatever the truth, the place of Sir Winston Churchill is assured within the history of the paranormal.

Churchill's psychic talents were undoubtedly instrumental in helping the allies to win the Second World War, though he would probably not have regarded what he did as 'psychic', because in a sense he just used his intuition. In other words, he was one of those people able to slip easily into synchronistic reality mode. As we have seen already, the fact that he was both an artist and a writer (and so naturally creative) helps explain why this was so. Such individuals seem not to be rooted in the concept that the world outside, unchanging and immutable, rules what we do; they habitually invent, create, alter and adapt within their minds to impose their rules onto the world outside. It seems to be this difference in symbiotic relationship between mind and matter, self and reality, which makes one either a sceptic (or psychic negator or traditional scientist) or a believer (or active psychic or imaginative artist). In astrology it is the difference between cold, hard-headed Saturn (or its sign of Capricorn) and sensitive, impressionable Neptune (or its sign of Pisces). There are shades in between, of course, but the truth still holds good.

During the Second World War, one evening Churchill was having dinner at 10 Downing Street when he inexplicably went into the kitchen and told his staff to leave and go to the shelter. There was a German air-raid on, but this was normal at that time, and it was standard practice to 'soldier on', which is exactly what Churchill did do. However, the staff obeyed his orders, and moments later a bomb detonated at the rear of the house, virtually demolishing the kitchen. His ability to switch reality modes and see beyond the normal boundaries of time probably saved several lives. Who knows how many other lives Churchill's wartime decisions protected?

I intend to return to the problem of time and premonitions later, but for now it should be noted how it appears to relate to this ability to move from one mode to the other, prescript events and so generate fortuitous 'coincidences'.

Let us return to the UFO enigma. I have written a number of books on this subject, and I am not about to repeat any of them by discussing what this phenomenon is. Suffice it to say that strange things are seen by reliable folk and something is – or more likely some things are – going on 'up there' which the authorities know only too well and have no real clue how to handle. There is even a House of Lords All Party UFO Study Group, based at Westminster, which I was honoured to address in December 1980. This group includes many illustrious names, such as the Earl of Clancarty and Lord Hill-Norton (a successor to Churchill as Admiral of the Fleet). Although it is rather unfairly portrayed in mildly jovial terms by certain facets of the British Press, the truth is that these men (and some women) are deeply interested in the reality of UFOs and seem bent on forcing the governments of the world to break what they interpret as a 'cover-up'.

Hill-Norton believes in such a conspiracy, although when he held the position of Chief of Staff at the Ministry of Defence he was not made party to it – which seems odd. He feels that there is a battle to get to the technological secrets of the phenomenon first. In this he is supported by some very powerful names (such as the chairman of the all-party Defence Committee, Sir Patrick Wall, a long-standing Conservative politician). Such people obviously lend credence to the UFO controversy. But I cannot help but ponder a strange scenario.

What if this mysterious upper echelon of power (maintaining this cover-up) were faced with the prospect of explaining to Hill-Norton why they had withheld information from him? For instance, a UFO might have surfaced in front of one of his warships, to be promptly fired upon, only to demonstrate such superiority as to pose a threat both to men and to their expensive naval hardware? How could such a foolhardy limitation of knowledge be justified? If there is a 'need to know' strategy, surely the head of the Navy or Chief of Staff at the Defence Ministry needs to know? To me it is both encouraging and yet problematic to see such people actively supporting the UFO movement. Yet it is hard to equate the evidence for a cover-up with the apparently remarkable selectivity of who administers that same conspiracy.

Over in France, in 1974, the head of the Defence Ministry, Robert Galley, issued a public statement saying he believed in UFOs and wanted a full-scale investigation (which was later funded, and still operates in 1985). But how come the Minister of Defence was not aware of 'hidden knowledge' about this nasty defence problem? And look again at the quote from Lord Dowding at the head of this chapter. Sure enough, Dowding also believed, but he too was claiming to have been excluded from the cover-up!

There is even a story rife in the USA that the CIA engineered a *coup* in a foreign country in order to preserve the secret. The Prime Minister of the state of Grenada, Sir Eric Gairy, had become quite a UFO fanatic, even to the extent of putting them onto his nation's postage stamps! He pushed and eventually won a debate on UFOs in the United Nations. This produced nothing much, principally because, as soon as it got going, its main champion, Gairy, was deposed. It seems he spent so much time in America promoting his UFO cause that he forgot about life back home (where he was not exactly popular). With his loss of authority at home he also lost all influence in the UN. Of course, rumour has it that the powers-that-be in those nations concerned with keeping the lid on the UFO situation saw Sir Eric as a big threat, so they aided in his removal from office.

Back in Britain even royalty have UFO interests. Earl Mountbatten, last Viceroy of India and uncle to Prince Philip (the Queen's husband) seems to have set the ball rolling. There are persistent claims in UFO circles that one landed on his estate and that entities conversed with a member of his staff. There is some evidence for this. And I even have my own Mountbatten tale to tell. In conversation with a former Lord Mayor of London some years back, I was told of a conversation he had had with Mountbatten. The gist of this was that the British had captured a spaceship, which was safely under guard at a South Wales air base. Quite why we have since wasted millions on follies like Concorde and the Advanced Passenger Train has never been made clear to me, since we now ought to be zipping between London and Edinburgh in a few seconds flat, courtesy of our Mark Two flying saucer. But no matter, the endearing tale remains.

Certainly Lord Mountbatten became quite a fan of the UFO mystery, reading its best-known journal *FSR* (*Flying Saucer Review*) before his untimely death, caused by an IRA bomb. He has passed on his keen interest: Prince Philip reads the magazine and takes an interest in the goings-on at the House of Lords group. Again I have to wonder why Prince Philip does not merely glance through those super-secret reports which surely *he* must have access to. Or are we to assume that this truly amazing cover-up excludes not just defence chiefs and military leaders but the Queen and the Prince too? If so – who are the mysterious manipulators of this conspiracy?

Like father, like son, they do say, and it seems that Prince Charles has continued this interest in all things strange. I am not aware if this extends to UFOs, but his support for alternative forms of medicine is now well known. And there are stories (which seem to have some foundation) that he senses the presence of his murdered relative, having made some attempts to get in touch with Lord Mountbatten 'beyond the veil'.

UFOs once played a part in the tragic end of one of the United

Nations' greatest statesmen, Secretary General Dag Hammarskjöld, who was killed in a still mysterious plane crash over Rhodesia on 18 September 1961. Witnesses on the ground reported that a strange object, like a small aircraft without lights, had appeared beside the plane before it exploded in mid-air. One said it was 'beaming lights on the larger aircraft. It was like a beam from a flashing torch'. There was on survivor of the disaster, US security guard, Harry Julian, although he soon died of his wounds. He told a nurse that just before the explosion he had seen a strange 'spark' in the sky at the side of the aircraft.

In July 1984 rather similar claims were made about the multi-million-pound fire which destroyed part of the historic York Minster. Here 'sparks' and 'beams' were seen to hit the roof, allegedly from a hovering UFO. However, careful investigation revealed that a form of rare atmospheric phenomenon was probably the culprit. Likewise in the Rhodesian air disaster: ball lightning, or some stranger electrical hazard, may have manifested alongside the plane and ignited the fuel tanks.

UFOs clearly exist in some form or another, but what about mysterious animals tramping undetected around this planet? There are those who feel they also exist and may have similar explanations. If we were to interpret these alien spacecraft as dreams originating not in a single mind, or one person's life field, but in the life field of the entire human species, could the Loch Ness monster or the Yeti have such a starting point? Or in even stranger vein could they be dreams of the fish and ape species field, as opposed to the human race? There is something rather delightful in imagining Nessie swimming around its cold, dark loch as a kind of collective nightmare from all the millions of fish in the world. To them it certainly would be a god of some description, taking the role that super-spacemen have for us *homo sapiens*.

Regardless of whether this is true or not, these monsters are seen by humans. The search for the beast of Loch Ness is now well documented, although it is only half a century since the first sightings occurred. Now it even has an official name, coined by the famous naturalist and son of the polar explorer, Sir Peter Scott. *Nessiterras Rhombopteryx* he has called it, meaning 'monster in Loch Ness with the diamond-shaped fin'. This was based on some underwater photographs which purport to show the enormous creature but which are believed by certain researchers to be shots of a sunken monster once used in a movie! It has also been pointed out that, with unfortunate irony for Scott, his chosen name is an anagram of 'monster hoax by Sir Peter S'.

Nevertheless, there have been persistent tales of large unknown animals in both lakes and seas for many years. By another Scottish loch Lord Malmesbury recorded in his diaries two sightings of what he termed the 'Lake Horse' in 1857. He related that the locals were very superstitious about this strange creature, but seems to have accepted its reality.

Such was the popularity of these legends that the great circus showman Phineas T. Barnum offered a $50,000 reward (a lot of money in 1873) for the capture of a sea-serpent. Doubtless he would have made all his money back very quickly, but sadly he never got the opportunity.

Like UFOs, these monsters seem to fade in and out of our planet with undue ease. In many respects they act like ghosts, or indeed like dreams – which may just be what they are. But on occasion some degree of physical evidence is left behind. In 1978 Lord and Lady Hunt made a visit to Nepal and were amazed to wake one morning and discover huge animal footprints in the snow around their tents. The natives knew what they were – the mark of the Yeti, or Abominable Snowman, a great hairy creature said to stalk the hill areas of several continents. It does look like a *real* animal, having white fur in snowy lands, brown/black coloration in the USA (where it is known as 'Bigfoot') and more grey/brown pigmentation in the rocky lands of Europe.

But are any of these things real? Or are they just quasi-real? They do seem to follow the trend of our cultural beliefs. The UFO which destroys a church in 1984 would not have been that in 1784, or 1584. What will it be in 2184?

This same cultural belief offers us a lovely tale to end on. In 1982 Wyoming rancher Pat McGuire decided to run for State Governor, as a member of the Democratic Party. This decision was prompted by a fleet of aliens who landed on his ranch and became about as commonplace as cattle (not that he ever managed to obtain any evidence of this, naturally). These alien visitors showed him how to dig a miracle well in barren soil and then pushed him into his historic political mission. With their guidance he waged his campaign, giving pledges such as the one which promised that, unless both the USA and USSR left the Lebanon to its own devices, the aliens would have to kick them out, regardless of the destructive consequences! His support from party colleagues was not exactly overwhelming. One offered the following words to a delighted media, 'Why does he have to be a Democrat?'

When the primary election came, McGuire did manage to poll over ten per cent, which was possibly a surprise, but he still lost by a huge margin to the resident governor. When asked for an explanation, political commentators laid most blame on the rancher's 'unusual campaign style'. Nobody is predicting what will happen if he stands again!

6. The Psychic Lives of World Leaders

'Who is dead in the White House?. . . The President. . . He was killed by an assassin' – visionary dream of Abraham Lincoln.

It is not all that healthy to be President of the United States. Of course, that statement could be made about any world leader, but it is especially true for the one whose destiny puts him at the forefront of American politics.

There is even what amounts to a jinx in the form of a twenty-year cycle which supposedly ensures that any president elected into office in 1920, 1940, 1960 (and twenty years back from then and forward into the future) will not survive their term (or terms) of office. They will instead die as President. Such a jinx would appear to be crazy. There is no obvious source or explanation for it. Unless one accepts that it is now such an engrained 'habit' or behaviour 'norm' that it acts like a curse on American society. Still it seems to work!

Astrologers have a theory that it is something to do with an opposition cycle in the heavens between the two planets Jupiter and Saturn (Jupiter being the planetary archetype for rulers and leaders, and Saturn the harbinger of death and termination). Long before President Ronald Reagan even entered the 1980 race, his demise was predicted. Other, more cautious astrologers pointed out that Saturn (the real baddie planet) was in a much stronger position than usual, which according to their rules should moderate its nastiness. However, few held back from their prophecy of doom. The outcome was attempted murder within three months of Reagan's taking office, but despite his age he survived the gunshot wounds. As I write this, he has won his second term, in November 1984. And the jinx now has four more years to work out. What price his survival through all of that? With madmen and old age, two unpredictable enemies, one cannot envy these projected months. Somewhere I have a sneaking suspicion that Jimmy Carter might not be all that sorry he lost out in 1980!

One of the earliest victims of the jinx was Abraham Lincoln, elected the USA's sixteenth President in 1860. Lincoln was, of course, a popular leader, noted as a humanitarian and for his fight against slavery. Of all the men to occupy the White House, he must surely rank as one of the greatest. On 14 April 1865 he had just begun his second term when he was murdered by an actor, John Wilkes Booth, as he sat in a theatre.

This tragedy was steeped in premonition, as if the fact that it was one of the greatest emotional traumas in the species field allowed a sort of 'seep-through' foreknowledge of the event. We might argue that in terms of morphic resonance such a massive effect on our life fields creates so much disturbance that it *can* be detected in advance much more easily by people who are temporarily occupying synchronistic reality mode.

In her memoirs Julia Grant, wife of US General and later President Ulysses S. Grant, records how she awoke on the morning of the 14th with a terrible sense of doom. She had a compulsive urge to get her husband out of Washington, but he had a meeting scheduled with Lincoln and so was very reluctant to leave. However, Julia Grant became very insistent, and finally her husband decided he could refuse her no longer. Although he had been invited to the theatre with Lincoln that night, he excused himself and left the city. On the way to the station they even apparently passed Booth *en route* to his deadly rendezvous. It was later revealed that General Grant had been on Booth's death list. But for Julia's powerful presentiment, history might record the loss of two great men on that fateful day.

Julia Grant was a noted psychic (another way of saying she could slip into srm rather easily). Lincoln himself often acted on impulse (intuition), like Churchill years later. The President even had visions of the future. We would recognize these as signs that he too could switch modes with more than customary ease.

In view of Lincoln's ability and the postulated existence of such a powerful effect on the species field, it should not be too surprising to learn that the President received a premonition of the drama in which he was about to star. He retold his vision (which he had on or about 1 April) three days *before* the tragedy. It was recorded by one of his aides and close friends, lawyer Ward Lamon. 'There seemed to be a death-like stillness about me,' Lincoln explained. 'Then I heard subdued sobs, as if a number of people were weeping.' He went on to describe how he roamed the White House searching for the source of the misery and came upon a terrible scene containing 'a corpse wrapped in funeral vestments'. He made enquiries of the invisible voices and was told that the body was that of the President, dead at the hands of an assassin.

An interesting question here is whether Lincoln had merely acquired information from the future of the species field and built a sort of imaginative reconstruction around this raw data for his vision or whether he previewed an actual scene in the White House (and his dream is not inconsistent with that possibility). That last option would seem to presume that some element of Lincoln *survived* death. Otherwise how could he know about something which took place later than when he ceased to exist?

A simple way of looking at this phenomenon, which I like as an illustration (although it is not necessarily a perfect analogy), concerns what I call the 'bow-wave' effect. When a ship moves, it pushes water out at the front and rear; ripples indicating this passage spread out in two different directions. If we imagine an 'event' (as a sort of crystallization of something from out of the species field) and time as a sort of energy within which this manifests, one can envisage 'ripples' surrounding this event cutting through time. The ripples which spread backwards from an event are easily recognized. The event creates an effect (greater or smaller) within the species consciousness. So these backward ripples reflect the 'after-effects', so to speak. It is not illogical to expect balance and to envisage bow-wave ripples moving forward into time. Such ripples would lie ahead of the event (as the ripples in water lie ahead of the boat announcing its coming to anybody watching).

After-effects in the species field would mostly be felt by way of changes in the emotional state of human beings (e.g. we feel sad and morbid after a death). Bow-wave ripples may well be emotional too, so that people who can slide into synchronistic reality mode will detect and visually dramatize them (probably in symbolic terms just as we do in our dreams). Of course, that suggests that emotional events will be much easier to detect. So major tragic affairs within the species field will be previewed far more often than minor happy ones. Studies into such emotive incidents (e.g. the collapse of a coaltip onto a school full of children at Aberfan, Wales, in 1966, or the sinking of the packed luxury liner *Titanic*) would seem to support that idea. Likewise, the death of Lincoln probably allowed many more people to detect the event beforehand than would the death of an ordinary old man who passed away from the combined effects of senility on the same date. We have two examples (Julia Grant and Lincoln himself) but there were probably others. And as you will see, the same process was repeated in this present century when another great President died suddenly.

This second death was that of John F. Kennedy, elected nineteen presidents later, in 1960. There are many similarities between Kennedy and Lincoln, sufficient for some (with rather more fancy than evidence) to propose that they are the same 'spirit' reincarnated. Certainly both were great civil rights fighters, extremely well loved, peace-makers and considered by many in the world to be potential saviours (not exactly standard fare for US presidents!). The fact that they were brought to office precisely one hundred years apart is an interesting 'coincidence' (and meant, of course, that Kennedy was already singled out as another victim of the twenty-year jinx). However, the links between Kennedy and Lincoln do not end here. They are decidedly weird.

Lincoln and Kennedy both died on a Friday by being shot in the back of the head whilst sitting next to their wives. Their killers are both widely known by a three-part name (John Wilkes Booth and Lee Harvey Oswald). These men were born a hundred years apart and neither came to trial, both being murdered before this could happen. Booth shot Lincoln in a theatre and fled into a warehouse. Oswald shot Kennedy from a warehouse and escaped into a theatre. Kennedy had a secretary called Lincoln. Lincoln had one called Kennedy. Lincoln was in the Ford Theatre when he was shot. Kennedy was riding in a Ford car (the model being a Lincoln!). Finally they were succeeded by presidents born a hundred years apart (1808 and 1908). Both were southerners, and both were called Johnson.

Our minds just lose control in the force of such stupefying arrays of circumstance. Can all of this be mere chance? In view of the other paranormal bonds between the deaths of Kennedy and Lincoln, I would certainly not count on it. The answer must lie somewhere in the species consciousness field.

Just as with Lincoln, Kennedy had a personal premonition. He told both his wife and an aide (as Lincoln had done): 'If somebody wants to shoot me from a window with a rifle, nobody can stop it. So why worry about it?' This may seem like a rather understandable speculation, even though it did turn out to be exactly correct. However, in view of the fact that these words were uttered just hours before Oswald fired his murderous shots, it looks more like a prediction than a guess.

President Kennedy's death disturbed the species field enormously, as shown by the glut of alleged premonitions. The number is enhanced partly because this death occurred in the TV age, when people felt they knew him, and partly due to the speed with which word of the assassination reached the homes of people even thousands of miles from Dallas, where he died. The after-effects of this ripple were felt far more deeply and for longer than any other single event in the decade (probably in the century). By reciprocity we would anticipate the bow-wave to be equally dramatic. It was.

Numerous claims of Kennedy premonitions exist. One previously unpublished example comes from Ann Phillips, a British housewife. The night before Kennedy was shot, she had a dream in which she 'saw' the US President driving in a car when three holes suddenly appeared in his head. Blood and brain matter oozed from the wounds in a supposedly gory picture. There was absolute silence associated with the images, but a terrible sadness and emotional heaviness. This again would be acceptable in view of what I said about the ripples being mostly emotional.

Ann did discuss the dream with some work colleagues on the Friday, but nobody took her seriously. And she did not identify the victim specifically to them, as she was not clear about this from what she 'saw'. It was evening in Britain when the terrible events occurred in Dallas. On returning to work after the weekend Ann was accused of being a witch. She is not. She can merely switch reality modes very easily, which probably has a lot to do with the fact that she has seen two very unusual UFOs (both of which she photographed!) right outside her bedroom window.

Probably the most famous of all Kennedy predictions stems from America's most celebrated prophet, Jeanne Dixon. If you write to Jeanne, as I have, you will receive back prayers and messages that demonstrate how deeply religious she is. Her ability to foresee future events is considered by her to be a gift from God, and to her credit she uses it wisely. But she is inevitably a media star.

As long ago as November 1944 she was called to the White House by the ailing President Roosevelt (who was elected in the jinx year of 1940, of course!). He wanted to know how much time was left to him for his grand plan to initiate the United Nations movement and bring an honourable and lasting peace to the world when the horror of war was over. As direct as ever, Jeanne says she told him, 'Six months or less.' He died of a brain haemorrhage in April 1945, just a few days before the war in Europe ended and his beloved United Nations got underway.

Jeanne Dixon's fame was created by this story, although she told it only after Roosevelt's death. But it was her pre-publicized visions about Kennedy that won her global status. She says that in 1952 she had a 'divine revelation' (her words for the most powerful class of visions she has) in which she saw the image of Kennedy outside the White House with the numerals 1 9 6 0 and a dark cloud which smudged and then rained onto the presidential offices. She knew then that the man elected into office in 1960 would die. Not that this was a particularly remarkable prophecy in view of the jinx.

Jeanne says that she has two quite different kinds of experience. Her ordinary visions are not so clear-cut and show events that can be avoided. Divine revelations, on the other hand, are master-plan events perfected by God, and their effects on the species consciousness are such that they cannot be prevented. The Kennedy murder was one of these. I am tempted to wonder if this might not just be an excuse to cover Jeanne Dixon's fallibility, for we remember her successes and forget her failures, although there have been many of them! She saw the disgraced Richard Nixon as a 'great President', and also predicted he would win an election he lost. She saw the White House flag flying at half-mast in 1983. And she predicted that in 1981 a terrorist would use a stolen nuclear bomb for blackmail. Such dramatic boobs provide precious little faith in her up-and-coming predictions (a woman US President before 1990, peace in Northern Ireland in 1988, and the commercial use of icebergs in 1985, when they will be towed by ship from the North Pole!).

However, it does seem that Jeanne Dixon (like most psychics who have ready-to-order predictions demanded of them) falls prey to accidental trickery. When the mind switches reality mode and detects emotions from a bow-wave ripple, it does this unnaturally. There may be a limited number of events which can be seen sufficiently far in advance to make publishing them worthwhile. Most would relate to events in the very near future, which are next to useless for a professional psychic. But also it may be that those who delve into the world of synchronistic reality again and again have difficulty telling the difference between its products and the more mundane results of imagination. Both are clothed in symbolism, since this is how the mind in srm operates. As astrologers would say, the planet Neptune (which is responsible for such things) rules both true psychic visions and imaginative fantasy.

Many of Jeanne Dixon's 'visions' probably reflect her own inner beliefs and aspirations. Only occasionally does she truly detect those ripples in the species field ahead of a major event. The Kennedy predictions seem to be one such occasion. She wrote of how a blue-eyed Democrat would win the 1960 election (well before Kennedy looked likely to stand), and as the day of his death drew close, her visions began to 'fine-tune'. The emotional ripples were stronger and more concentrated now (as they are in water when closer to the boat). So the construction of the coming murder was now more sharply defined. She did try to warn the President, even though she 'knew' there was nothing she could do about it. That apparent contradiction is nevertheless what we might expect from someone utterly convinced by her visions and desperate to do something to avert the catastrophe she has foreseen. Her phone calls, letters and morose murmurings to friends led her nowhere and probably never reached Kennedy, although one of his aides is known to have tried to stop him going to Dallas on that November day.

Just as we found with British Prime Ministers, so too with American Presidents: the UFO mystery has become a decided thorn in their sides.

Gerald Ford, before he ascended to high office and while he was in the Senate, determined to force the issue in 1966 after a wave of sightings in Michigan. Hundreds of people had observed weird, dancing lights, and there was quite a furore. Matters were scarcely helped when a governmental adviser announced (at a hastily arranged press conference) that the lights were probably due to 'swamp gas'. The media had a field day! The chances are that this explanation probably *was* valid in certain cases, but it was never seriously proffered as a general conclusion. Not that the local people cared about that. They were after blood, and Ford championed their cause. He did eventually force a commission, at which media star Carl Sagan sat in deliberation and suggested a funded research project manned by several universities. In the end one university took on the job and concluded that UFOs were bunk, despite failing to find answers for one in three of the selected cases studied.

Officially Gerald Ford seems to have been satisfied. At least when he became President there was not a peep out of him about 'flying saucers'. But another politician was finding time to take an interest, in between peanuts. Jimmy Carter had just seen a UFO! In fact the flickering light which so baffled the former naval officer was almost certainly just an astronomical body twinkling through the earth's atmosphere, but it was strange enough to send him off on a mini-crusade about the reality of the phenomenon. He echoed Ford's by then forgotten words and told the American people that they had a right to know the truth about this great mystery. Indeed, he made it a focal point of his campaign when he entered the race for President in 1976.

Carter won the election, and you might be wondering what happened to his pledge. Political promises are not always kept, of course, but in fact Carter did keep this one – up to a point. That is, he asked NASA to launch an enquiry into the phenomenon. I have a copy of a letter (leaked to me by a serving American Air Force officer) which shows NASA reacting internally. A USAF colonel was advising them in September 1977 that he sincerely hoped NASA would refuse Carter's request. A few weeks later they did just that – risking potential repercussions on the already tightly squeezed space budget. It seems to me that you do not refuse a request direct from the President to use money he is offering to conduct a research project. Especially when that request concerns an election pledge and is from a President who believes he has seen a UFO himself. At least not unless some other factor intervenes.

I understand that that other factor was a private briefing Carter was given by intelligence staff. This supposedly introduced him to the political dynamite of the UFO phenomenon. The source of this information, a White House aide, says that Carter had to be stopped from pushing for public access to information. So it was explained (and proved) to him that UFOs were alien craft piloted here by a race who more or less control the planet. They had been responsible for our cultural, religious and scientific progress. They called the shots for the future. We were mere pawns in their decision-making. Even US presidents were just puppets. How true this all is I do not know, but Carter also stopped talking about UFOs. When NASA said no, he accepted their refusal and quietly dropped the whole matter.

Just what was Jimmy Carter shown to change his mind so dramatically? Perhaps it was the same thing which two decades earlier another President, Dwight Eisenhower, is said to have confronted.

The Eisenhower tale is a legend in UFO circles but has some evidence in its favour. A week after returning from holiday in February 1940, Eisenhower suddenly disappeared off on another one, to Palm Springs, California, which just happens to be a couple of hours drive from Muroc Air Force Base (now the Flight Research Centre at Edwards Air Force Base). This was long reputed to house the remains of a crashed UFO captured in 1947, along with several of the dead aliens! The stories about this are surprisingly consistent. Then for several hours on 20 February Eisenhower went missing from his Palm Springs trip. The Press, who follow his every movement, realized the importance of this, and all kind of rumours flew around, including one which suggested he had died! Later an impromptu press conference was called in which a pretty weak tale about 'emergency dental treatment' was offered. However, the family of the dentist allegedly involved seem rather reluctant to confirm what ought to be a proud moment in their lives – if it were true! Alongside this little mystery are reports from several sources on the base which insist the President did pay them a secret visit that day. He was allegedly shown the UFO and the aliens, possibly because he (like Carter) was trying to tell the public the truth.

Obviously this sounds fantastic and virtually unbelievable, but many statements now exist, collated by American investigators, and including sworn affidavits, confirming this incident, the original crash and the autopsy and other work on the aliens and their UFO. It seems hard to believe that they are all unfounded.

It may be hard to swallow, but according to Beverly Gleason, wife of famous American TV star Jackie Gleason, it is all true, because she recalls a night in 1973 when her husband arrived home late and slumped into a chair, ashen-faced. 'I've seen the bodies of some aliens from outer space,' he claimed. Gleason was a good friend of then President Richard Nixon and is known to have had a deep interest in UFOs. Nixon is supposed to have personally set up the visit to the Air Force Base where the four beings were. According to Beverly, they were only just over two feet tall, with bald heads and unusual ears. This sketchy description is very similar to the one offered by all others who are said to have seen them. Jackie Gleason himself has refused to confirm or deny the story.

Are all these claims mere fabrications? If not, the proof of alien reality does exist. And yet it is being obscured by one of the tightest security operations ever mounted. That can only be happening if there is a very good, probably rather disturbing reason.

Edward VIII, the King who abdicated his throne because of his love for a divorced American lady (thus entering exile), had one of the most eventful royal lives of recent centuries. If the bow-wave effect does occur, it is just the kind of thing which would trigger it into action. Love, turmoil, sacrifice and sadness are all great emotions which must have made their mark on the species field. We might expect many detections of the ripples leading to apparent predictions of the chain of events. Indeed, there are such reports.

The great French prophet of the sixteenth century Michel de Nostredame (or Nostradamus as he is best known) seems to have described the loss of King Edward VIII's throne with the following words, from two separate verses: 'The young one was born to rule Britain, which was offered him by his dying father. When he is long dead, this subject will be discussed. And from his son the rule will be demanded. For not wishing to consent to the divorce, which will thereafter be regarded as unworthy. The king of the isles will be forcefully driven out. And in his place will be put one who has no sign of rulership.' This does seem remarkably apt, including the reference to George VI, who had to take on the task his brother was forced to leave. He had never expected to become king and had no real desire for the job.

Much closer to the time of the constitutional emergency precipitated by these events, two astrologers on each side of the Atlantic made intriguing predictions. Evangeline Adams in New York told Wallis Simpson, the woman who would cost Edward his crown, that in a 'serious emotional crisis' she would 'exercise considerable power. This power will be related to a man.' Meanwhile in London Cheiro was predicting the future of the then Prince of Wales and foresaw changes which would 'greatly affect the throne of England'. He called the future king 'restless', said he would have difficulty settling down and suggested that he might well 'fall victim of a devastating love affair'.

This all does look like powerful evidence in support of the reality of bow-wave ripples in the species field, which can give warning of major events that will stir up our consciousness, especially in an emotional way.

Assuming that this is true, we ought to be able to find evidence for any great event that is looming ahead of us now. What would be the consequence of a third world war, for example? The emotional ripples from that might fairly be imagined as horrific. And if you take a look at the predictions of the many psychics who have been noted for some successes (and thankfully some failures!), the theme of nuclear/biological warfare on a catastrophic scale is a very dominant one. I will not go to any great lengths to assess the mountains of data. But I feel I ought to offer a few 'highlights'.

An Irish archbishop (later St) Malachy, in the twelfth century, produced a list of mottoes for each of over a hundred popes he said were to come. He supposedly got these from visions. Over the centuries many of these seem to have been accurate, leaving one bemused as to how a man eight centuries back could possibly come up with such phrases to describe men not born.

Recently, for instance, there has been Paul VI, motto 'Flower of flowers' – his coat of arms was a fleur-de-lys, followed by John Paul I, the Pope some claim to have been murdered, motto 'From the middle/half moon' – he died after only thirty-three days in office – i.e. between half moons. John Paul II succeeded him in

1978. His motto is 'From the labour of the sun' – *'De labore solaris'*, in Latin. Nobody has accurately assessed this yet. But it is interesting that the Pope is Polish (the first from a Communist country) and that he has become associated with the 'Solidarity', movement amongst the labour in that nation, symbolizing liberalization. I have been accused of rather forcing the Latin to equate *"solis"* (sun) with *"solidarity"*, which is fair enough, but the labour implication is clear enough.

How long John Paul II will reign remains to be seen, but after him comes a pope with the motto 'Glory of the olive' (which may mean the olive branch – i.e. peace-making). However, what is more ominous is that after him there is just one other pope left on the Malachy list! He is 'Peter of Rome', and Malachy penned a much longer script about him. He said that he would be the pope who will guide his people through 'great tribulations', when the final apocalyptic war strikes. This will destroy Rome and ruin the Church. He is last in the list because there will be no more popes after him! Reasonable estimates would place this drama as towards the end of this century. But, of course, it could be earlier – especially if Jeanne Dixon's predicted papal assassin succeeds in his ambitions.

In the fifteenth century a farm boy from Cheshire made dire predictions about the future and spoke of the next time England's shores would be invaded (yet to happen). This would be by a nation 'with snow on their helmets' and who 'shall bring plague, famine and murder'.

One hundred years later the great French prophet Michel de Nostredame wrote his cryptic 'centuries' ten sets of verses which aim to give the list of coming attractions for planet Earth. His supporters claim spectacular success, but this often depends on how liberal you are willing to be in your interpretation of his vague words. Sometimes he gives dates, and for the next two decades he appears to talk of both nuclear and germ warfare wiping out whole cities and killing millions – although the earth survives (you may be pleased to hear). His datings seem to place the start of these troubles (when an 'easterner' decides to 'come out from his seat') as the mid/late eighties onwards, with the real battles early in the nineties and the war culminating in 1999 (a date he gives quite specifically).

Then we have the prophecies of Fatima, Portugal, given in 1917 to some peasant children by a visionary figure they assumed to be the Virgin Mary. These are apparent predictions of the ending of Word War I the rise of Russian Communism, the start of World War II and so on. A mysterious 'third prophecy' was offered but has been held by the Papacy for many years and never released publicly. Unofficial versions say that it speaks of the destruction of the Papacy at the end of this century, following a third war in which 'fire and smoke will fall from heaven, the waters of the oceans will become vapours' and 'millions and millions of men will perish'.

The pattern is self-evident from all of this and (of course) we all hope it is just doom-mongering. But can we be sure? Despite all our rhetoric and arms limitation talks, the knowledge of how to build nuclear missiles and biological weapons will never go away. And there is not a means of destruction ever invented that man has not one day found a reason to use. The Earth also has a habit of producing the occasional lunatic who one day soon is bound to find himself in the position of being able to use these horrors.

If such an event were to happen, it would be unimaginably powerful. The emotional suffering of millions must deeply scar the species field. Presuming that premonitions are fact (and I must do that from experience), the choice is quite simple. Either there will *not* be a great war and so no long-range ripples, or there *will* be one, and these ripples will already be evident. One could interpret these ancient prophecies as the first weak detections by extremely gifted people able to switch reality modes. If this is so, we ought to see more and more evidence in the world around us of concern, fictional reflections and premonitions about nuclear holocaust. I fear that we are seeing precisely that.

It is a long way from Abraham Lincoln to the near destruction of Earth, but both are linked by the bow-wave effect. Its study leads one into waters that threaten to sink you beneath unthinkable possibilities. We have a curious trust in our futures, liking to believe ourselves immortal. But none of us is that. However, the future is out there waiting for us to meet it. Perhaps even now it is rippling back its warnings of the horrors to come. We are fools if we ignore them.

7. Writers' Inspiration

'When I take my pen . . . I am as much a medium as Dunglas Home . . . When I write a play, I do not foresee nor intend a page of it . . . The play writes itself' – George Bernard Shaw (playwright).

Once upon a time there was a wonderful story-teller known as Edgar Allan Poe. When he sat down to create a tale, he would empty his mind and just let it fill to the brim with ideas, sometimes weird and wonderful, sometimes rather grim.

One day he decided to write a story about a shipwreck and the dreadful plight of its survivors. Cast adrift in an open boat were a small collection of desperate men and a cabin boy. Dipping into that pool of subconscious imagery somewhere in his head, Poe dredged out the name Parker. That was a fine name for the poor lad who would be both hero and victim of this macabre lament. So in need of food would the mariners be that they would find themselves forced to kill and then eat the boy. Having written his tale, Poe sat back satisfied. And soon he was off writing another one. The story of the cabin boy's terrible demise languished on the shelves for many years. Then suddenly it all came true! There was a real shipwreck. One survivor was a cabin boy named Parker and as the food ran out he was chosen as a sacrifice to keep the rest of the men alive.

Edgar Allan Poe had created many fictional masterpieces, but never before had he created future reality. His novel was *The Narrative of Arthur Gordon Pym*, published in 1833.

This anecdote would be strange enough were it unique. But it is far from that. In fact I have experienced things rather like it myself. So too have many writers, as well as creative and artistic people whose minds tend to enter synchronistic reality mode more often than most.

Singer Peggy Lee says that sometimes she and her band seem to join minds and become one unit. If she misses a section out of a song, as she is carried away on emotional euphoria, so do her fellow musicians. There is no conscious link between them all. At the level of the species field they are pooling their resources and acting as one. This is how telepathy seems to occur. Minds resonate at the level of the species field. Once in a concert Peggy suddenly found herself thinking about an aircraft. She could not get the image out of her head, and it almost spoilt her performance. It was only when she returned to her dressing-room that she learnt that a dear friend had been on board a plane which had just crash-landed. Fortunately nobody was seriously hurt, but her friend's trauma had somehow transferred itself into her mind, presumably because she was in synchronistic reality mode at the time.

Indeed, when you are engaged in some short of inspirational pursuit, this does appear to facilitate that change of state. Writers, when they try to compose, often 'free-wheel' and so find themselves able to access bow-wave ripples from a future event. In this way they may pick up information about something destined to occur, but think that it is just an imaginative creation of their mind. If they write it up as a novel or short story, like Edgar Allan Poe, then when the situation later comes to pass, the novel looks decidedly eerie. I call this process psychic parallelism, and it is very common. By some psychic means the writer creates a fiction which later parallels reality.

Bow-wave ripple detection may be the true explanation in most cases. But when a novel or story is very powerful, it too might stir up the species field and focus not unlike a curse. As a behaviour habit it might then be responsible for turning fiction into fact. Indeed, in psychic parallelism both things might operate together.

I was delighted to learn that science-fiction writer Ian Watson regards his only UFO novel (*Miracle Visitors*) as rather special, because when he was writing it he suddenly found real UFO sightings occurring all around the place where he lived! (I could cite several other examples I have found from the chronicles of famous writers, but I guess it is even more common than all of this suggests, although writers generally shy away from mentioning it – which is easy to understand: they are not to know it is the way the universe operates.) Watson's novel centres on the intriguing idea that UFOs are like a dream born out of the species field. His story stems from Jung's archetypes and from speculations by a French ufologist, Bertrand Meheust, who first saw hints of psychic parallelism between UFO reality and science-fiction.

I think we can synthesize some kind of theory from all of these speculations and experiences. Creative minds are able to see ahead and detect bow-wave ripples from coming events. Possibly based on these they are also able to prescript behaviour so as to manipulate apparent 'coincidences'. If their creation is sufficiently powerful, it may itself initiate a new behaviour field which may come to affect the norm. As Sheldrake says, by the law of habit the idea will now crystallize out as a fact.

Those who serve as the artists of our world must accept their responsibility, for an artist does not just portray what is: in a very real sense he causes it to be. Creative people are the architects of reality.

We may now have found the explanation for the UFO phenomenon (or that part of it which is not to do with types of natural energy such as UAPs). It would also explain why it has changed throughout history. And indeed it may furthermore explain all paranormal 'myths' (such as the Loch Ness monster, Bigfoot, phantom big cats and so on). They are creations of the species field, brought into being by habit. We believe in them enough for myth to become reality, and fiction to be fact.

In UFO terms, where did the mystery airships of 1913 go? What happened to the 'foo fighters' (strange blobs of light which chased aircraft during World War II)? Why did disc-like spaceships suddenly arrive in 1947? Why is the latest 'invention' of the UFO phenomenon abduction by aliens (with memory repressed until hypnosis)? Such things did not exist until the 1960s.

Researcher Rodney Jones has come up with the name 'Cultural Tracking' for this phenomenon. It is absolutely correct that UFOs track our culture and technology but never predate it. In my previous book *Alien Contact*, I discuss how the home planet of the aliens has traversed the universe in keeping with our developing awareness of the most likely abode of true extra-terrestrials. If you examine the reported insides of any UFO encountered two or three decades ago, you will find not a single laser, hologram or electronic display. They all follow the pattern of *Star Trek* episodes filmed twenty years back, on which the equipment on the amazing 'Starship Enterprise' consists of cumbersome number counters clicking away and computers which then looked compact but today seem like monolithic giants. If the UFOs in the phenomenon we perceive were *real* spacecraft, surely they would contain technology which took rather longer than a couple of decades to be made redundant by our primitive science? This all rather implies that the appearance of a UFO is conditioned by our ability to imagine the appearance of a UFO.

The UFO phenomenon may be one of the best examples we have, in true working action, of an aberrant response in the behaviour field. In June 1947, when the first modern UFO was seen (and it matters none what that really was), the media spread it so rapidly and it became so important to our society that many people began to search the skies for 'flying saucers'. A lot found them. Because this new behaviour field quickly became dominant, it turned into a habit. It was now easy to see UFOs, because to do so had become a norm. I suspect that in some peculiar sense the combined effect of all this belief and observation actually brought them into existence.

In my first UFO book, with Peter Warrington, I suggested that some UFOs were a psychic phenomenon 'conjured up' by psychokinesis. I have never lost my belief that UFOs are essentially a subjective *experience* (as opposed to an objective *observation*). We now have a way through any awkward magic tricks. UFOs will continue to exist for as long as enough people want them to. This must have something to do with the fact that UFOs have declined markedly since Speilberg's Hollywood movie about them. It seems to have blurred the distinction between dream and reality. It has also taken away the need of many to see UFOs in the sky, now they have seen them on the cinema screen. It has possibly begun the death of the UFO phenomenon.

Will the UFOs return in a new guise? Probably. For we will always need some sort of mystery, to act as a kind of mandala for society to concentrate upon. As soon as some phenomenon achieves sufficient popularity to turn from an aberrant behaviour field into a norm, that experience will become a habit rooted within the species field.

We can see how this happened with metal-bending. Prior to the arrival of an Israeli magician-cum-psychic called Uri Geller, apparently nobody was able to bend iron bars and cutlery with the power of their mind. Yet as soon as he demonstrated his ability to a wide enough audience, it was suddenly common-place. Geller's fame created a new habit in the species field, and it was now quite easy for people to bend metal. This would apply whether Geller was a genuinely talented psychic or an outright hoaxer. It was the belief in him that caused the change, not his authenticity.

Of course, you must appreciate that when I say that it is 'easy' to see a UFO or bend metal I do not literally mean that everybody can do it, but I do suggest that for people able to slip into synchronistic reality mode it becomes an 'in vogue' way of expressing their new range of abilities. All of this supports the contention that some new phenomenon will come along, gain widespread promotion and then, as one British comedian likes to say, 'You'll all be doing it tomorrow.'

Let us now explore a little deeper the borderline between fiction and fact, prediction and creation. A classic example is the saga of the *Titanic*.

In 1898 writer Morgan Robertson penned another in his series of sea novels. This one, *The Wreck of the Titan*, told how the allegedly unsinkable luxury liner the *Titan* sank in mid-Atlantic after striking an iceberg, and how its insufficient supply of lifeboats led to terrible loss of life. Fourteen years later fiction became remarkable fact when the unsinkable *Titanic* went down in just those circumstances.

Next we move to 1935 when a third ship, the *Titanian*, narrowly escaped the same fate when struck by an iceberg in the same part of the Atlantic. A crewman born on the very day the *Titanic* sank had a premonition of disaster and helped warn his navigator in time.

You might think this is sufficient action for any aberrant in the species field, but the *Titanic* disaster has become such a habit now, thanks to books, movies and so forth, that we shall probably find its theme repeated through the years to come. Bob Rickard, editor of a delightful collection of mysteries, *Fortean Times*, has already given us one example. In Bedfordshire in 1975 while a family were watching a TV showing of a movie about the sinking of the *Titanic*, a huge chunk of ice fell out of a clear sky and smashed through their roof. One wonders what will be the next trick up the sleeve of the cosmic joker.

That brilliant pioneer of science-fantasy Jules Verne was extremely gifted at creating reality. It is thus not difficult to see why his novels became so popular. Just as Ian Watson would write about UFOs, and UFOs would then hound him, so Verne wrote about mysterious airships and they started to appear. His stories *From the Earth to the Moon* and its sequel *Round the Moon* have got to be amongst the most amazing examples of psychic parallelism. They predate the Apollo missions by one hundred years, yet there is so much about them which mirrors reality. His launch site was in Florida, very near Cape Canaveral; his space mechanics (of orbits, speeds, times of flight etc) turned out to be astonishingly accurate. However, strangest of all is the way these novels seem to have prescripted the near catastrophe suffered by Apollo 13 in 1970. In Verne's story an oxygen explosion prevents the spaceship *Columbiad* from landing on the moon, so instead it has to use a remarkable 'slingshot' tactic to catapult itself back to Earth. It crashes into the sea, and its fortunate crew are rescued by a ship in the Pacific.

When NASA chose the title *Columbia* for their third lunar lander, they were tempting providence. When flight 13 went up at 13.13. CST, it must have seemed like an omen. Then two days later (on 13 April of course) an oxygen tank explosion prevented the landing, and the world held its breath as the crew used a 'slingshot' tactic to fly around the moon and catapult itself back to Earth, to be rescued by a ship from the Pacific. This was just what Jules Verne had already written. It is perhaps more fortunate than we can ever know that he was a lover of happy endings.

So far we have examined many examples of creative people switching reality modes. But what do we do when this happens? It seems that to enter srm you need to alter your state of consciousness. For this purpose we should consider a spectrum of reality.

At one end of the spectrum lies waking, objective, everyday experience (normal reality mode). At the other there is the sort of subjective experience we undergo whilst asleep. This is synchronistic reality mode. But there are types of reality of all shades in between, which blend from one extreme to the other and contain greater and lesser degrees of both reality modes. One of these things is the lucid dream, where the dreamer *knows* that he is dreaming and can somehow control the subjective landscape of the dream. On the principle that the spectrum must be balanced, we might predict a mirror image of this, a sort of 'waking lucid dream'. This takes place in a situation regarded as objective, where the person knows that he is awake and can somehow control the landscape of the real world. He can make miracles happen: bring aliens to life, print Yeti tracks in the snow, allow the Loch Ness monster to be photographed. This is the Quasi-Conscious Experience.

Some illustrations of this phenomenon will help. Pamela Mason, the actress wife of movie star James Mason, was going out with a man after her divorce. They had a fight and he left, apparently with no intention of returning. After some hours she desperately wanted to talk to him again, but she had no idea where he would be. Drifting off to sleep, pondering this question, she suddenly found herself dreaming and yet aware. The knowledge of the whereabouts of her lover entered her mind, and she *knew* where he was. In the morning she telephoned him at an inn which had a very unusual name and which she had not known existed before her Quasi-Conscious Experience. He was there.

Another instance is reported by the actor De Forest Kelley who plays 'Dr McCoy' in the *Star Trek* shows, who often gains information by way of his dreams. In one he saw William Shatner (who plays the hero of the films, 'Captain James T. Kirk') holding a clapperboard with some figures and a dollar sign on them. He guessed these to be Shatner's salary, a secret closely guarded from other members of the cast to avoid jealousy. The next day he told Leonard Nimoy (who plays the alien 'Mr Spock'). Nimoy knew Shatner's salary, and the figures dreamt up by Kelley were almost exactly right.

I use the shorthand 'QC Experience' as a handy way of referring to this kind of phenomenon. It is essentially a descriptive phrase for the range of different paranormal events which can occur when a person is temporarily in synchronistic reality mode – events which are in ordinary eyes 'impossible' and which include the detection of bow-wave ripples about the future, sensing changes in the species field caused by emotive happenings which affect us or our loved ones, and prescripting the way that we handle reality so that 'coincidences' are forced into being.

In the quote which heads this chapter we saw how George Bernard Shaw tended to undergo a QC Experience. He would sit quietly and let information pour out of his subconscious mind or from the species field itself. Data that he would neither realize he possessed nor comprehend that he had access to would then be moulded into his plays. They more or less wrote themselves. We have seen this same thing described by other writers, such as Robert Louis Stevenson. It is frequently remarked by authors or poets who seem bemused by the mystery of inspiration. In ancient times it was even thought that 'muses', or little spirits, were responsible for transmitting this material. When George Eliot or George Sand found themselves facing up to it, they tried to discover more rational solutions. There is a rational solution, but it has to be seen in vaguely paranormal terms until we truly grasp the different layers of reality which structure our universe. That marvellous poet William Wordsworth well summarized it when he spoke of 'That awful power rose from the mind's abyss, Like an unfathomed vapour that enwraps.' He knew the magic of inspiration from the species field.

Richard Bach, a pilot who wrote one of the best-loved fairy-tales of the twentieth century *(Jonathan Livingston Seagull),* went further and was able to put it to remarkable use. He recognized that he was receiving information from a source. He did not believe it was himself, or the species field, nor did he invent a muse, but he did believe it came from something external. This seems to be a common way in which the mind copes with the inflow of strange impressions and information. It transposes them to an outside agency to deny responsibility. Often the exact nature of this outside source is largely hallucinatory. Uri Geller regarded his source as a giant computer in outer space! In all these cases the true source is the wellspring of consciousness (or the species field, or in UFO terms maybe even a sort of universal consciousness), but we dress it up as a spaceman, dead humans or super computers.

For Richard Bach, his inspiration was at first just a 'warning voice', not unlike that described in connection with Winston Churchill. It saved him from disaster in a split-second mid-air situation on at least one occasion. Later he came to regard the flow of information as a message from an overflying seagull (although it was not quite that simple!). Certainly he was able to create a remarkably vivid account of the life of a seagull, told from the point of view of its consciousness. Bach said of his 'non-fiction' book, as he insists on calling it: 'I'm the writer not the author. I did not invent anything of that story. I didn't originate any of the actions that happened. But I did write it down.' I think by now you should be able to grasp what he means.

Ernest Hemingway, the great novelist, had his switches in the form of an OOBE (Out of the Body Experience), something which Richard Bach also went through on occasion. It is a fascinating phenomenon in its own right and involves a person suddenly finding himself floating 'outside' his body, and possibly even viewing it down below him. From the new vantage point he feels free of all the normal reality-mode shackles and can wander through time and space in the typical sense of srm. Often such events occur spontaneously during illness or accidents, and there are sufficient cases on record to indicate that at times information is obtainable that would not be available to the mind (when located 'in' the body) at the spot where it is physically situated.

Zoologist Lyall Watson, for example, in a bus accident 'saw' during his OOBE a young boy trapped by the wreckage. Later, when he was back 'in' his body and hauled out of the smash, he found that the boy was precisely where he had viewed him, although he could not have known that from where his body lay.

I have had one pretty undramatic OOBE myself, so I can speak from personal experience of its strangeness. I was terrified by it and quickly snapped back to normal reality 'inside' my body, which is probably why this is the only such experience I have had.

Bristol psychologist Dr Su Blackmore believes that the OOBE, whilst a fascinating phenomenon (she has undergone many of them herself), is basically imaginary. This matters little, since the state is clearly a QC Experience and allows access to information by non-standard means. The image of floating and externalization from the body may be another trick of the mind to cope with the switch into the new reality mode.

How do you tell what sort of experience should be termed QC? Are there any clues to look for? There are indeed. I have gathered them together under the umbrella term 'Oz Factor'. They include statements from the percipient similar to these which follow: 'It went strangely quiet – all sounds just disappeared'; 'I seemed to be floating half in this world and half out of it'; 'Time seemed to slow down and stand still.' The witness feels as if he is taken out of this world and into another, where magic can happen. The term 'Oz Factor' comes from the way in which 'Dorothy' and 'Toto' get transported by a whirlwind to the fantasy land of Oz in the classic fairy-tale.

Watch out for the Oz Factor. This signifies that somebody has undergone a QC Experience, during which they will have switched over into synchronistic reality mode – where almost anything might have happened!

A fine illustration of what this chapter has been about is the incredible symbiosis between Stephen Donaldson's recent phenomenally successful *The Chronicles of Thomas Covenant* and the real-life events claimed in the strange book *The Green Stone*.

The Covenant chronicles are told in a series of six very long novels by Donaldson, a young and previously unpublished author. They describe how a modern American, Thomas Covenant, and a doctor, Linden Avery, are transferred into an alternative world where they have psychic powers and can perform magical feats. This world is populated by strange, mythic creatures, and after gathering together a team of them, they set off on a quest which involves discovering a green stone and a small sword, to fight a cataclysmic battle against a force of evil. The books were published between 1977 and 1983 and have been huge sellers, topping the lists on both sides of the Atlantic. Their effect on the species field is therefore not difficult to discern. And to be such a success they must have resonated with a need within our society, following the 'time is ripe' principle I outlined before, such as in the discovery of Neptune.

Contemporary with this (and certainly I and many others knew of these events early enough for us to be persuaded they are not fabrications based upon the Donaldson novels), a group of real, ordinary people began to gather together in Britain to follow a quest, and found that together they had strange psychic powers. Off they went in pursuit of a green stone, which they found after first discovering a small sword buried inside a crumbling bridge. Using these powers, they had to fight a cataclysmic battle against a force of evil.

The psychic parallelism between the 'fiction' and the 'fact' (as told in the book *The Green Stone,* by quest members Martin Keatman and Graham Phillips) is amazing. I cannot possibly give more than a hint of it here. The allegedly 'true' story is so incredible that few people will believe it when they read the book. But I was fortunate enough to be working with all the people involved while writing *my* book *Alien Contact,* which is a sort of 'prequel' to the saga of the stone. I was not involved in the quest in any way, but I saw enough to be sure that it is not all lies or delusions. In some way and in some sense it happened.

We might interpret this as the enormous popularity of the Covenant stories somehow creating a behaviour norm, out of what are interwoven mythic elements which must have already had some pre-existence in the species field. Then a group of people slipped into srm and together (on the basis that the whole is greater than the sum of its parts) formed some sort of harmonious liaison. As they were in a QC Experience, the reality they acted out was only quasi-real. But as with flying saucers or Loch Ness monsters, or any other consequence of the QC state, the result is tantalizing. It is illusive and subjective but tinged with real overtones. The sword and the stone which were found are like the physical traces left by a UFO. They are all that solidifies out into our absolute reality from the quasi-real experience the members of the quest underwent.

It may be that with most of these phenomena you need to *be* there in order to understand them. Or you need to be there for them to be real.

8. Musical Mystery Tour

'A star fall – A phone call – It joins all: Synchronicity' – from the song 'Synchronicity' by Sting of 'The Police' (musician).

From what we found in the last chapter, it ought to come as no real surprise that musicians are significant for both psychic parallelism and shaping of reality. They have a mass influence over people (especially young people, whose minds are easier to destabilize because they are less set into habit). Radio repeats the same tunes over and over again, and the listeners perform a metaphorical tribal dance, synchronizing themselves with the rhythm. It is the closest thing to brainwashing yet invented!

Not that I am a denouncing modern music. I trust any younger readers will not perceive that in my words. I often use music as an aid to concentration or creativity myself, but I do keep a careful watch on its subtle effects and also how it reflects current philosophy, using the same sort of 'cultural tracking' we found in terms of the UFO phenomenon.

One of my favourite stories concerns the heavy metal group Iron Maiden. Their famous song 'The number of the beast' has as a chorus the number 666 often repeated. This is the ancient and Biblical sum afforded to the Antichrist. (It has always intrigued me that the great fire which destroyed much of London, then the centre of the world, happened in 1666, and that we use 999 as the British emergency telephone number when 111 would be quicker to dial. This is probably the source of those holocaust predictions

94

for the year 1999).

The group had a tough day at the studios getting that track laid down, thanks to minor problems constantly cropping up. Then on the way home their producer was involved in a serious car smash. He survived but when he recieved the garage repair bill was astonished to find that it had totalled up to £666.66p!

A considerable proportion of modern 'creative' musicians (by which I mean these whose lyrics are rather more meaningful than 'Yeh, Yeh, Yeh') have regularly produced songs whose themes centre on the paranormal, the way information of a cosmic significance is obtained by way of srm and warnings about the future of planet Earth. You can almost provide a musical soundtrack for the ideas in this book if you put them all together!

Jeff Lynne of ELO (Electric Light Orchestra) seems to know full well what I am talking about when I refer to the species field as a source of inspiration, fiction and quasi-reality. In his songs (probably composed whilst he is in srm), he often talks of how things come 'out of the blue'. For example, in his 'Secret Messages' (1983) he calls it 'a moving stream of information that is floating on the wind. The secrets never end. And now they call, they sing, they play, they dance.' On the same album, of which this is the title track, he seems to explain how the QC Experience can crystallize out of such a contact. In his 'Time after Time' he asks us to 'Just listen to the sirens of the world' because, as he puts it, there is 'no hiding anywhere' from 'the visions in the air' which 'come from everywhere'.

There is even a branch of music known as 'Cosmic Rock', where the lyrics are deliberately chosen to express profound ideas. The Moody Blues were one of the founders. In 1981 Justin Hayward suggested in 'The Voice' that we 'Make a promise, take a vow, and trust your feelings. It's easy now. Understand the voice within, and feel the changes already beginning.' Here he tells us how to gain access to those Jungian archetypes or to Sheldrake's species field by tuning into the 'voice' – the same 'voice' which allowed Churchill to save his staff from the bomb outside his kitchen, or Abraham Lincoln to visualize his own destiny.

Kate Bush is another singer who has views about and experiences with the paranormal. She has even been the president of one UFO group. On a 1978 album she advises us: 'Don't fall for no magic wand' because 'We humans got it all – we perform the miracles.' And in 'Kite' she tells how it feels to enjoy QC reality care of an OOBE: 'I got no limbs, I'm like a feather in the wind.' Kate Bush has also penned what might well be the anthem for any anomaly researcher, in her 'Strange Phenomena'. This speaks about the way synchronistic reality can produce prescripts and coincidence: 'You pick up a paper, you read a name. You go out, it turns up again and again.'

As the quotation at the head of this chapter shows, one of the world's most successful ever groups, Police, are intrigued by the same phenomenon. I cannot resist describing a truly amazing adventure I had in connection with their music, whilst I was in the midst of my radio series in April 1983.

I had chosen to do the following week's Radio City programme about coincidence and srm and called it 'Synchronicity', although I had to explain this for the benefit of my listeners. The day before I announced the next week's show at the end of the current week's programme, I had a rather strange 'phone call' telling me all about a 'star fall' over Merseyside. (Look at Sting's lyrics on p. 94!) What I learnt from my terrified caller was that a strange object had been seen coming out of the sky at 4 a.m. that day (it now being about six hours later). He was certainly upset about it, so I decided not to press the matter on the phone, but a few hours later I heard on the Radio City news that two young boys had been killed in that same Merseyside district during the preceding night. They had abandoned their motorbikes for no obvious reason and crossed a nearby railway line on foot, where they were struck by an oncoming mail train.

My curiosity was piqued by this tragedy, and when I went to the radio station the following day, I checked the news teletype file on the incident. I was surprised to find that the accident had been not just at the same place but also at the same time as the UFO sighting which had been phoned through to me. Now I had an unusual decision to make. Should I call the police and tell them what I knew, thus in a way implicating both myself and the innocent UFO witness in the sad death of these boys? It would also necessitate facing ridicule for even daring to suggest any sort of connection with 'flying saucers'.

Another complication was the fact that I had just emerged from half a day 'helping the police with their enquiries', as they say, after a thief had chosen to dump a getaway car that had been involved in an armed robbery right outside my front door in the middle of the night! This made me even more reluctant to return to the police. However, reality was already beginning to conspire to tell me what to do. Or probably I was prescripting reality, because on a deeper level my mind already knew what it wanted to do.

I was in the studio with presenter Brian Ford, having completed the show and announced that next week I would be telling listeners all about synchronicity. I chanced to remark to Brian that discussing synchronicity in front of tens of thousands of listeners was quite likely to push the phenomenon into action. Now I was seeking his advice on the episode which had occurred over the past twenty-four hours. As we talked, during a break whilst a record played, we could see through the glass panelling into the radio station's reception area, which allows visitors to watch the DJ perform his work as the shows go out live. In walked two police officers in full uniform! Brian and I smiled to one another, and I said 'See what I mean?' They had actually come to interview another DJ about unpaid fines, but for me it was rather more pointed!

If I had any doubts about what I was being told to do, they disappeared as I left the studio and walked across Liverpool to catch the bus. *En route* I stopped to buy a record, and with my purchase I was given a free magazine that reviewed records and previewed those coming up for the next month. Topping the list, as I discovered reading the magazine on the bus going home, was the brand new album by the Police, which was to be called *Synchronicity*! (Later, when it climbed to the top of the charts in May and June 1983, I found the lyrics of the title track and the way they were so pertinent to my curious brush with this phenomenon.)

Now I had no choice. I called the police when I got home. Without telling them about these synchronicities, I merely passed on what I knew. Nobody seemed to think this silly. A few weeks later (by 'coincidence' of course), I was picked up in a car as I walked through Wallasey, heading for Liverpool to do another radio show. My lift came from a plain-clothes police officer who recognized me and who listened to my show whilst on patrol. We got to talking and it transpired he was involved in the mysterious death incident and added that the theory of the boys having been frightened by a UFO, dropping their machines and fleeing in front of the train was as plausible as any other they had to go on!

Doubtless you will find all of this rather hard to believe. I find it difficult enough myself. But as Police say in their song: 'If you act as you think, the missing link [is] synchronicity.'

The record I purchased on the day I discovered the forthcoming *Synchronicity* album was by Al Stewart. He is another singer/song-writer who talks much of weird phenomena. He has produced a whole album around the theme of 'Time' and a long track about the prophecies of Nostradamus, amongst much else of note.

On a 1984 album there is a track, written by himself and Peter White, entitled 'Rumours of War', which neatly coincides with points I made in the previous chapter. If you recall, I suggested that people who are sensitive enough should be able to detect bow-wave ripples from events destined to affect the species field in a big way. One such event is a forthcoming horrific war and, as we saw, there are signs (in the growing concerns, fictional accounts and population movements) that early subliminal detection may be occurring. 'Rumours of War' is about exactly that, and its being released after I first drafted these chapters provides a good example of either psychic parallelism or the 'time is ripe'pattern we have met before.

In their usual poetic style Stewart and White say, 'I can see you're one of that kind who carry around a time-bomb in your mind. No one knows when you'll slip the pin.' And indeed I am sure there are many such people on this planet today who do contain those dreadful warnings locked up in their heads like a time-bomb ticking away. As the song adds, 'There are souls on fire in the day and the night – on the left and the right – in the black and the white. You can see it burn in the eyes of the rich and the poor – rumours of war.' That this refers to true paranormal presentiment (not just fear) is shown by lines such as, 'You tell me just look all around. . . . The signs and the planets are lining up like before.' My guess is that we shall see many more songs such as this in the years to come as this bow-wave ripple grows stronger and stronger.

I hope that we heed the warnings before it is too late. Time is desperately short, or else we would not have so much evidence.

Many people have another way of gaining temporary refuge in synchronistic reality. They use an ancient Chinese oracle known as the 'I Ching'. It is basically a list of sixty-four 'readings', each quite detailed (and with sub-readings within them). The words are pretty vague (not unlike Nostradamus's predictions) and one can see many things in them. To gain access, you just throw a set of three coins six times and according to whatever combination of heads and tails 'chance' dictates, a specific reading is recommended for you. You then read this as the answer to the question you had in your mind as you tossed the coins.

Of course this is crazy. A bunch of coins and some mumbo-jumbo written by an ancient Chinese sage centuries ago can hardly interpret your future or respond to your enquiries (however serious). Still, despite all of this, it seems to work! But you must be sincere and ponder the question in a state of meditation as you throw the coins. The I Ching is just an aid for slipping into srm which is easy for some people to use. And you probably have to be in srm when you read the words of the oracle and extract from here the ones most relevant to your enquiry.

Pop singer Marianne Faithfull used the I Ching at a time when she was girlfriend of leader of the Rolling Stones, Mick Jaggar. In June 1969, when the Rolling Stone Brian Jones had got himself heavily into drugs and had quit the group, she consulted the oracle. She cast number 29, K'An ('The Perilous Pit'). Her interpretation of what was written can be synthesized as danger/water/a pit/death. She tried to warn Jones, without success. A couple of weeks later, whilst under drug influence, he fell into a swimming pool (an archetypal perilous pit of water!) and drowned.

I think you need some susceptibility for entering srm in order for this to work, but if you successfully meditate whilst employing it (and meditation is just another route into synchronistic reality), it can probably be of value. But it must not be overdone. Part of its success lies in its reverential flavour.

Let us look at some examples of phenomena which have happened within the musical world which serve to illustrate ideas we have discussed so far.

On 16 August 1977 Stu Brunner, a Missouri radio disc jockey, tried to play an Elvis Presley record on his station KFAL, but he could get neither side to work. The needle just slid over the record groove. In the end he gave up and put on another record. A few minutes later the station received a bulletin to transmit: Elvis Presley had just died. Later the record was examined and found to be undamaged. It played quite normally.

Now what do we assume happened here? You might be

inclined to believe that the spirit of Elvis paused on the way to the after-life and decided to have one final giggle at the expense of the world. Frankly, this seems ludicrous, even if the after-life were an established fact. However, what if Brunner had been lulled into srm by being cooped up in the studio with music playing continually and softly in the background? What if in this state he was able to realize that the pop star was dead? (This may not have been by precognition, but most likely simply detecting the changes in the species field which the event was already beginning to create as Presley's death became known.) In synchronistic reality the message would be understood. But it is very hard to seep this through into normal reality. Perhaps the simplest way opportune at that time was to mess up Brunner's normal co-ordination (certainly a normal reality, subconscious mind function) thus preventing his putting the record on correctly.

Three years after this episode Alex Tanous, a well-known American psychic, was interviewed for a radio show called *Unexplained Phenomena*. He discussed his visions and told of a feeling he then had that a 'very famous rock star will have an untimely death'. Anticipating my views about the bow-wave ripple of a major event being due to its greater effect on the species field, Tanous added, 'It will affect the consciousness of many people because of [this man's] fame.' On air he said little more, except that he felt the star was living in America but was not an American. Privately, so he claims, he drew up a list of six candidates. Top of this was former Beatle John Lennon.

The radio programme was transmitted in October 1980. On 8 December that year John Lennon, having just returned from a recording session, was murdered outside the apartment in which he lived in the Dakota Buildings on West 73rd Street, New York. Across the road and overlooking it was the radio studio where Alex Tanous recorded his prediction!

Lennon would not have been surprised at this. He had had several brushes with the paranormal himself. In his hit single 'Strange days Indeed', released after his death, he says: 'There's UFOs over New York – and I ain't too surprised.' This was a cryptic allusion to his own close encounter, some while before, when he observed a cigar-shaped object over the river. (We shall meet Lennon again in Chapter 12.)

John Lennon is by no means alone in having had such visions.

The group Hot Chocolate wrote their number-one chart success 'No Doubt About It', which discusses the reality of UFOs, following a sighting they made on the way back from a late-night performance. As we saw, the UFO phenomenon is a very much 'in vogue' way of expressing your talents once you enter srm.

I have even established a lively UFO communication with a delightful lady in the USA. Some years ago she and her young child underwent a dramatic encounter with a landed UFO which appears to have been what an investigator calls an 'abduction' (there were elements of missing time). It ought to shock nobody that she is a remarkably gifted artist, who now produces beautiful paintings of UFO phenomena as visualized by her and who has also experienced other 'paranormal' phenomena. Both of these things are major clues that show a person who is able to change reality modes with unusual facility. Since the experience this witness has changed her name deliberately to Judith Starchild. She has begun to write music (mostly about peace, love, harmony and the deeper meaning of life in the universe). I have a copy of her first studio 'demonstration disc', with her group Phoenix, and suspect that one day she will be a great success. For the day seems to be coming when her message will make sense.

That great pop star from the sixties Gerry Marsden, who was head of the smash-hit group Gerry and the Pacemakers, is another UFO witness. His encounter on the Wirral peninsula, just a short ride from Liverpool on the ferry across the Mersey, involved mysterious white lights which danced about his car when he was travelling near the village of Clatterbridge. When I talked to Gerry about this experience, I familiarized him with the concept of UAPs, or strange atmospheric effects. He was not aware of such ideas and had been brought up with the traditional view that you either had to be mad or had witnessed a spacecraft when you reported sighting a UFO. However, he was willing to accept that the UAP idea made sense in the light of what he had witnessed.

Another Liverpool group, but of what is termed the 'New Wave', has also had some rather strange confrontations with the UFO mystery, although they seem to regard their contact as with an alien intelligence. The group is called 'A Flock of Seagulls' and has had several hit records, including 'Run' which talks of fleeing from the bright lights in the sky. In another song they describe some of their own space messages with the title 'It's not me talking'. They refer to the information as coming from 'another planet'. It is not altogether clear to me whether they truly believe this or not, but what they talk of has many similarities with Uri Geller's super computer. Undoubtedly information is being transmitted to suitably receptive minds and is offering basic concepts about the need to end wars and stop fighting. It may be a super intelligence elsewhere, or it could be those mysterious inner regions of ourselves, the species field.

I think that these cases of information transfer or prediction have one thing in common. Synchronistic reality functions on the basis of symbols, not concrete facts or logic as does normal reality. Using tea-leaves, a crystal ball, the I Ching or astrology to foretell the future is just a way of bridging the gap between the two realities. They are the symbols which translate the data coming to the mind in synchronistic mode (which can be bow-wave ripples from the future). They crystallize them out into our everyday reality. The same may well be true of the messages spelt out in the songs our creative musicians produce. That the information stems from some real source is undeniable. That this source is an alien one, or at least an intelligence external to man, is not yet proven. But this hardly means that we should ignore their voices. That they are so loud and insistent probably means they speak great truths.

It has doubtless occurred to you that, if we can detect bow-wave ripples from major future events and dramatize them as symbols, dreams or hallucinations, the same may be true of information from the past. An interesting tale involving some popular musicians in the days before they became stars is worth recalling in this regard.

In a party travelling from a concert late at night on a quiet road in the south of England were Peter Bardens (who later went on to keyboard fame with the group Camel) and Mac Fleetwood (who was soon to form the internationally acclaimed Fleetwood Mac). Whilst driving they spotted a figure on the road ahead, but they were so close that they could not stop in time. Despite screeching brakes they crashed right through the spot where the man had been standing. Oddly they felt no bump or sign of collision, but they were sure that they must have hit the wandering stranger and probably killed him. The frightened musicians stopped, to get out and look around. The pedestrian was nowhere in sight. It was only later that they discovered he was indeed dead, but he had died long before they hit him. A man had been killed on that stretch of road some years before, and legend had it that his apparition was sometimes seen to haunt that spot.

In other words these men had run over a ghost. But just what is a ghost? Are they detections of information from the past of that location? Do they occur when the people involved are in synchronistic reality mode? Lonely roads at night are certainly conducive to lulling the mind and teasing it away from its normal operations. But just how real is a ghost? We must explore this further.

9. Spooks and Entertainers

*'. . . reality and belief systems are virtually synonymous.
You have no reality other than your own belief systems'* –
Edgar Mitchell (US astronaut).

Actress Susannah York is an international star who had a very
strange brush with this mysterious world a few years ago. At the
time she was house-hunting with her husband, and on a friend's
recommendation they went to inspect a sixteenth-century house
in rural Essex. As Susannah was making a movie at the time, they
could pay only a flying visit but the owners agreed to let them
stay in the unoccupied property overnight. Arriving late and
giving it a quick inspection, they instantly fell in love with the
place. The house was like something out of a fairy-tale. It even
had a moat with its own drawbridge, which was the only way
into the building.

Despite her attraction to the house, Susannah awoke that night
from a deep sleep and suddenly 'felt' a presence all around her.
She got out of bed to explore but was overcome by a powerful
surge of emotion. Something was wrong. She could not move.
She felt dreadful and sensed an awful doom. Her body reacted to
all of this in the most natural way: Susannah York fainted.

The noise brought her husband to the rescue, but she remained
out cold for several minutes. In the morning, apparently
recovered, Susannah dismissed the experience. She was still
keen on the house, and so they decided to return at the weekend
for a more leisurely examination of the premises. But once more,

despite the beauty of the place, a growing overpowering sensation enveloped the actress. Feeling trapped, she announced that she could simply never live there. If the drawbridge ever broke down, the only escape would be by jumping into the waters of the moat. That was too much to bear. When the vendor heard this decision, he told the couple that he was not surprised. The house had a ghost. A young girl had been trapped there when the drawbridge had failed to operate. Desperate to escape, she had leapt into the moat and drowned. Her presence had often been sensed around the place.

Another British actress who had trouble whilst house-hunting was Corale Browne. In 1950 she actually bought a London home (adjacent to a graveyard!) which was to prove disastrous. Soon after they moved in, events began to plague Corale and her husband, and even their dinner guests on occasion. Plates and saucers would speed across the room under their own steam. Objects would also vanish for weeks on end, only to reappear exactly where they had been prior to their sudden disappearance. After eighteen months, convinced they had a poltergeist (or 'noisy ghost', as the word means, due to their noted capacity for this sort of mischief), the couple decided to sell up. It was learnt that in the decades before and after their tenancy the house could never keep an owner for more than a year or so. It must have been too problematic to have a spook for a lodger.

There are interesting parallels between these two cases. Susannah York merely detected emotions. In Corale Browne's house they were projected into some sort of physical destructive reality.

Energy of some sort must be involved in such phenomena. They cannot just be products of the imagination. The strange experience of the popular comedy duo 'The Krankies' demonstrates this. Their act revolves around Janette Tough, a dynamic little Scots lady pretending to be a small boy called 'Jimmie', who is always getting involved in all kinds of trouble with a grown-up, Janette's husband Ian. They have progressed from nightclubs to television stardom.

The Krankies will probably never forget New Year's Eve 1978, when they had to fly from pantomime in Newcastle to Scotland, where they were due to perform in a live television programme. The BBC chartered an aircraft for them, but the weather had closed in and snow covered much of the north. However, they had to get through, and the pilot decided that his modern instrumentation would take them there. As they flew on, a strange white object suddenly appeared above them. It hovered on top of the aircraft, whose instruments began to malfunction. Bravely the pilot struggled on as the brilliant UFO continued to pace them. Then, after several minutes of this close confrontation, it flew silently away. The aircraft's electrical equipment was now operating normally, and once they had touched down, it was easy to persuade themselves that perhaps the weather had been responsible for upsetting the gauges. Or perhaps not. The connection with the mysterious object seemed very hard to deny.

There had been a re-entry by a Russian satellite booster rocket that evening, and it had caused a fantastic sky spectacular around 7.05 p.m. But was this what the two entertainers saw? The time appears to have been later, and the hovering they reported is quite inconsistent with the rapid descent through the Earth's atmosphere of some space junk. We shall probably never know. But UFOs have often been reported as scrambling electrical equipment, even stopping car engines. There have been other occasions where aircraft have undergone similar effects when an object was nearby. Are they all just coincidence, or is there some peculiar energy involved with the phenomenon?

At least 'The Krankies', as true professionals, went on with the show as if nothing had happened.

We might be tempted to conclude that what Janette and Ian Tough witnessed was a sort of externalized hallucination, perhaps using the fact that some space junk was around. Does it bear close similarity with the hallucination of a ghost, built up out of data received by minds in synchronistic reality? There were Oz Factor symptoms in the mid-air encounter, just as there are in many apparitional experiences. This means that once more we have to accept that we are dealing with something that is quasi-real (a QC Experience) and not absolutely real.

Actress Anne Baxter can help us to understand this more fully. She is perhaps best known to most people in Britain for her starring role in the TV series *Hotel* and it may not be realized that she is the granddaughter of the famous architect Frank Lloyd Wright. They lived well apart but were very close, a bond which seems to have been important because it allowed their life fields to resonate or link together on synchronistic reality.

When Wright became ill, he battled through his illness, and

Anne Baxter had no real fears about him. However, one night she found herself having a dream choked with sad emotions. It was strange, but very frightening. The key element was a huge bird that was flying away from light and heading straight for her. Just as it approached, she awoke with a start and got out of bed. Such was the impact of the bird images that it took her an hour before she could calm herself down again and switch off the light. Just as she had done so, the phone rang. It was her mother calling to say that Frank Lloyd Wright had died, about an hour before. He was living in Phoenix, Arizona, at the time. What seems to have occurred is that Anne had somehow detected the effect of her grandfather's passing, thanks to its impact on the species field and the emotional ties between them. As she was asleep, dreaming and in synchronistic reality mode, her mind had to use symbols to spell out the message. The giant bird, perhaps what her mind interpreted as a phoenix, and its flying away from light trying to reach her, seem very appropriate.

Again we notice the great significance of emotion in all these cases. What would have happened had Anne Baxter been awake rather than asleep when Frank Lloyd Wright had issued this emotional cry? It would probably have depended on whether she was tuned in to normal or synchronistic reality at the time. She is not herself noted for being 'psychic', which means she probably does not enter srm that often, but she might have sensed something, if the contact had been strong enough, just as Susannah York seems to have detected vaguely what had occurred in that house, but not sufficiently well to create any apparition of the dead girl.

Corale Brown did not harmonize with the information that surrounded her. In this case her life field and that of whatever was responsible for the presence in her house clashed with one another. The result was a sort of 'psychic noise', the poltergeist effects which occurred. Physical energy was certainly present, just as it was in the aircraft flown by 'The Krankies', or just as it is when a haunted room goes cold. Since a basic law of nature says that energy can never be created or destroyed, just change from one form to another, this is what we seem to be discussing: emotional energy being transformed into physical energy (such as heat or sound), and in other cases the reverse of that process.

Edgar Wallace was a famous British thriller-writer whose mystery stories have been the basis for many films and TV programmes. He was not a fan of the paranormal, although according to American researcher Charles McArthur there were those who tried to make him one, because of Wallace's vast public. Sir Arthur Conan Doyle as we saw earlier in the book, a leading Spiritualist and 'spook-hunter' tried to coach him as his successor, but the writer declined and waged a battle in print (when he was a newspaper editor) against an erstwhile friend who did support the movement. Both men were stubborn and had large egos; neither would apologize to the other. But one day in 1931 something very odd happened to end the quarrel. As Edgar Wallace stayed up late writing another scathing attack on the paranormal, he heard a voice call out of nowhere that he ought to feel ashamed! Later, so he says, he found the draft of this manuscript burnt in the fireplace, although he insists that nobody went near it. And finally, it now being almost dawn, he observed a spectral figure seated in one of his chairs. He recognized her as the dead sister-in-law of his spiritually committed friend. After smiling at him and offering condolences, she vanished into thin air. Edgar Wallace refused to discuss the incident, after writing about it, so we can never be sure he was not jesting. But the effect of this ghostly vision was real enough, and he said of it, 'I shall no longer sneer at spirits.'

Assuming it did happen, we are best advised to look at his experience in terms of a dramatic hallucination projected by his mind into the room in order to have great impact. A feeling, or strange dream, would probably have had little effect on Edgar Wallace, who was much too sceptical. Deep down, his unconscious mind knew that it had to be something very dramatic to succeed. And it may have realized that an end to the feud was in his best interests. So it extracted information out of the species field and reconstructed events and circumstances which could not be explained, including a ghostly apparition.

Ghosts are probably just extreme cases of a Quasi-Conscious Experience.

Edgar Wallace, being a sceptic, very likely spent most of his life in normal reality mode. As an example of somebody quite different, who finds herself in synchronistic reality mode frequently, we can turn to the film star and actress Lindsay Wagner.

Lindsay enjoys playing parts concerning the paranormal. In her role as 'The Bionic Woman' she was possessed of fantastic powers. In the movie *The Two Worlds of Jennie Logan* she played a psychic who could detect information from the past and eventually control reality to such a great extent that she slid into that past and prevented a historical tragedy. In the QC experience resulting from her ability to switch reality modes, the character she adopted was able to restructure the universe to her personal advantage. It is ironic that she found herself acting out this concept, for in truth Lindsay Wagner has exactly that ability! She has undergone countless very strange encounters with the paranormal and has said of the things that happen, 'I trust my psychic feelings and have often used them to guide my career.'

Lindsay's life is a most intriguing one, typical of the remarkable psychic she undoubtedly is. Her most important experience was one which saved herself and her mother. They were booked on an American Airlines DC-10 flight from Chicago's O'Hare Airport on 25 May 1979, but before boarding Lindsay picked up a terrible feeling: a very strong bow-wave ripple was coming her way. She insisted that they cancel their booking and take another plane. Fortunately for them both, her mother was used to Lindsay's 'intuitions' and so agreed without hesitation. The DC-10 crashed seconds after take-off, when it lost an engine. Everybody on board was killed, inside a horrific fireball. It was the worst plane disaster on American soil. Somehow Lindsay's mind had picked up the ripples from over two hundred people's life fields as they saw themselves wrenched from the physical world in an instant of unimaginable terror. Why she was lucky and the rest of the passengers doomed is a question we cannot answer. But how many of those passengers felt unusually ill at ease, or had vague premonitions upon which they chose not to act?

Actors are very sensitive people because they have to be able to shape themselves into different roles. Astrologers relate this ability to Pisces and the planet Neptune, as we have seen (actors are thus artists of the persona). Since this overlaps with the ability to switch reality modes, it is not at all surprising that there are many stories of weird phenomena emerging from the entertainment industry.

Lindsay Wagner is a remarkable example, but not unique by any stretch of the imagination. However, she does show us how, when a person enters srm they can adopt a variety of guises. We have seen how her future dreams and her detection of emotional ripples are two possibilities. In another instance she underwent a remarkable out-of-the-body experience. It was at a time when she was working on her *Bionic Woman* TV series and was physically exhausted. Resting on a settee, she floated up above her body and, in her own words, 'felt a strange sense of isolation'. This is one Oz Factor symptom, a sure sign that she was undergoing a QC experience. Another was her peculiar distortion of time. 'I thought the experience lasted a matter of seconds,' she says. In fact she was 'woken up' by a worried friend who had entered her house when he saw her flat out. She had been there prone for TWO DAYS!

In different circumstances, as we have already seen, somebody might have decided that Lindsay Wagner had been abducted by a UFO. Regression hypnosis would then have been employed to discover what had 'really' happened in this missing time. But in the QC Experience, time just does not exist in the conventional sense of the word. We know that from our dreams. When does it ever seem that we have been away from normal consciousness for eight hours? Rarely, if ever. One night it may seem subjectively like days and another just a blink in the eyes of time.

The experience of another TV star, Erik Estrada, who plays a motorcycle cop in the series *Chips*, is one more example. His mother called from the other side of America to warn him to be careful whilst riding his bike in the California sun as the show was filming. She had just seen him come to her in a dream and sensed great danger. A few days later Estrada had a spectacular smash whilst shooting a scene (so spectacular they actually used it on air!). He almost died. It is interesting that when in hospital and still critically ill, Estrada also entered srm and experienced himself out of the body. He was able to view his body on the bed with all his relatives surrounding it. Then he decided that he was too young to allow himself to die, so he climbed back into his 'shell', and from that moment on his recovery to full health was assured.

Was this another dramatized externalization, such as we have met several times before (e.g. with Edgar Wallace)? Or are some OOBEs real, in the sense that there is a way in which the life field can separate from the physical atoms of the body?

In her autobiography, the great ballerina Dame Margot Fonteyn tells how she experienced synchronistic reality, when she identified with the emotions and thoughts of another person.

When her husband almost died after being shot, she felt his life slip away and then be dragged back from 'heaven', even though she was not with him when this was happening.

Such 'crisis' sensations are very common, especially when two people are emotionally very close to one another. In other words their life fields are closely intertwined, and at the time of death or serious injury for one it sometimes proves possible to relay this information from life field to life field. It does not even seem to be restricted to the human species field, as other animals appear occasionally aware (by what we might call paranormal means) of distress felt by their young or their mate. And there are countless tales of a dog or cat being apparently aware of the exact moment when its human master dies.

Telepathy is probably not the transfer of anything from one place to another. It is more likely the synchronization of one life field with another. If you place swinging pendulums side by side, they will gradually share their momentum and end up swinging in harmony. This is doubtless how it works with minds. Mind A synchronizes with Mind B, so that they think the same and feel the same. This looks like thought-transference, but it is really life field harmonization.

In a large proportion of these crisis cases the phenomenon is externalized. There is a visual apparition of the person who is dying, for example. In one case which I followed up, a woman received an auditory (but not visual) message from her dying husband miles away. For her it was a phone call. Only when she put down the phone at the end of the experience did she realize that she was holding thin air. The house was not connected to the telephone!

As we saw in the last chapter, there is a tendency for us to blame an outside source for messages received internally which seem to us to be paranormal. We create super-computers or alien beings to take on the responsibility. If this is possible, it hardly seems unlikely that we could not 'create' very convincing visual images of a dying husband or wife in order to give more impact to the message we receive in our minds. After all the source *is* in a way external. And synchronistic reality is where imagery rules.

We have referred to Susannah York's detection of information about the tragic incident in the old house. Here she only 'sensed' the emotion. But what would have happened if she had visually externalized it? Her mind might well have painted a fairly accurate picture (although perhaps with overtones of Ms York's imagination) of that young girl from another century. If you like, she would have seen a ghost.

Actress Judy Carne was educated at a theatrical boarding school in Sussex. One night, as she was looking out of her window as she got ready for bed, she saw a young girl with long blonde hair and an old-fashioned blue dress standing beneath a large oak tree. Judy took in a lot of detail from her experience as the girl looked upwards at the sky and then walked out of sight around the oak. The next day she described what she had seen to her headmistress. That description matched the one of a young girl who had sheltered from an electrical storm beneath that tree many years before. The tree had been struck by lightning and the girl killed. As a memento of this event the tree still bore the scar, burnt into it by the energy from the sky. But some other kind of energy, of a psychic or emotive nature, seems to have burnt itself into the species field in a similar way. It has recorded the last few seconds of that girl's death. Judy Carne must have entered srm and detected the information about the event. She had then created a visual hallucination to represent the scene. I say hallucination, but this must not be taken to imply it was pure imagination. It does seem that some hallucinations can be built out of very real things, thus it would be more accurate to call them by their true name: apparitions.

In Judy Carne's childhood she saw many apparitions. This is not unusual – for two distinct reasons: children seem more able to dramatize visually information received during srm and so in one sense we call them more imaginative and in another better able to view apparitions. It is also true that a person tends to experience either no apparitions or quite a few of them. This implies that to have such an experience is a question of ability, not one of luck or chance. Either you are able to switch reality modes, or you are not.

Television actress Pat Phoenix, once of *Coronation Street*, certainly can switch modes. In this way she has experienced many apparitions, mostly in the form of ghosts. At her home in Sale, Cheshire, she had repeated visions of an old lady whom she believes to have been an actress from long ago. This harmony of life fields between the living and dead woman was probably relevant. However, many visitors to Pat's house allegedly saw the figure too, so it was not a figment of her undoubtedly creative mind. It was always seen dressed in the same way and carrying what looked like a bowl of soup.

Now if a ghost were a spirit of the dead, it seems very strange that they should allow themselves to repeat the same action again and again as if they were stranded in time. One assumes that even after death the life field is the *life* field, and not the equivalent of a zombie or robot. If not, then the afterlife would be a pretty terrible place. This similarity to a piece of looped film repeating over and over on the cinema screen of the haunted location rather supports the idea of a visual dramatization of information received by the channel of the mind.

The reality of phenomenon is well explained by Pat Phoenix herself, who says of her resident spectre, 'She [looks] absolutely solid. I couldn't see through her like they say [you should] . . . there was no fading. . . . One minute she was there, the next she'd gone.' Which is exactly what you would expect. The apparition is supposed to represent the *real* person. And real people do not have white sheets over their heads, or look like transparent plates of glass. They look like real people, and so should a ghostly apparition.

Edgar Mitchell is a US astronaut who, when he was on the moon, had a profound experience which has changed his life. 'It was an explosion of awareness,' he says. He went through what he calls 'a fusion of consciousness . . . a oneness with all that is'. In other words, he appears to have had a strong QC Experience in which he touched the essence of the species field, and maybe even something beyond that. If it is true that we have a hierarchy up from individual consciousness to species consciousness, we also probably have a planetary and a universal consciousness beyond. Indeed, universal consciousness may not be very different from what the various religions call God.

Mitchell now studies psychic and consciousness phenomena instead of flying in rocket ships. He believes answers will be found much quicker that way. He is seeking a new model for the universe and is of the belief that mind and matter are intimately woven together. This is a view that many modern physicists would not much quarrel with. For Mitchell there is no such thing as mind over matter. Consciousness is a integral part of the way in which reality is created. What we believe in sufficiently, we perceive. What we perceive is what is. Since matter is a part of what is, we can argue that matter exists because of mind, and not, as most scientists would argue, the other way around.

Our encounters with the world of the paranormal seem to be telling us loud and clear that science has it wrong. Mind is not just an advanced biological concept invented by evolution as the latest by-product of matter. Mind is very probably the constructor of the cosmos.

10. Hollywood's Psychic Lives

'There are other realities that are just as important as the
realities of the intellect' – Shirley MacLaine (film star).

It is somewhat comforting to know that when Agent 007,
super-spy James Bond, faces the paranormal, he responds just as
you or I would. Of course, I am referring to film star Roger Moore,
who plays the part in the movies. When he awoke at two in the
morning to find an eerie luminous mass at the end of his bed, he
did not administer a karate chop to its ectoplasmic nether
regions, nor did he exorcize it by way of a flame-throwing
cigarette lighter: he panicked, as anyone would, and was
thankful that it vanished just before it came upon him.

Ah yes, but 'Dr Who' – surely he would have no problems
facing something from the unknown? After all those battles with
cybermen and daleks, what could possibly terrify him? Well,
something certainly did terrify actor Jon Pertwee, who was the
Doctor for several years. When he was a youngster, staying with
a friend at an old Sussex manor house, a nasty thing took place in
his bedroom, a little-used room, which he had to occupy, to the
apparent concern of the house's owners, since there was no space
elsewhere. In the middle of the night young Jon awoke with a
dreadful feeling of ill, and he was instantly sick all over the
bedclothes. Shame-faced, he washed them as best he could and
said nothing the next morning. But the following night he was
woken again, and this time he discovered the reason for his

115

nausea. An awful smell of rotting flesh filled the air, and at the end of the bed was a greenish, vile mass which seemed to be made up of bubbles. This time the boy was not sick. He wet the bed instead. Then he fled out of the room in terror. Later he was told that people were always sensing and smelling things in that room, which is why it was little used. But they had hoped that a youngster would be able to sleep soundly enough not to be disturbed.

The visualization was probably a childish nightmare image, plucked from Jon Pertwee's subconscious. It is unlikely that a green thing was actually there in the room, but it may have been the way in which his mind dramatized in the external world whatever putrid, sickly horror he had detected whilst in srm. It is interesting that the bubble-like or corpuscular texture of the thing is a very common description of entities such as this. It is not clear what this means, but it appears to be a clue of some sort.

TV cop 'Kojak' – movie star Telly Savalas – was allegedly very baffled by a real-life incident that they dare not have invented as a case for him to solve. Nobody would have believed it! He claims that, when his car ran out of petrol and he was hiking down a lonely road through a forest at three in the morning trying to find a garage, suddenly a car appeared and he was offered a lift. The driver lent some money to Telly for him to purchase petrol, and the actor insisted he must repay it. To this end the man scribbled down his name, address and phone number. Later, when he called the number to arrange to pay off the debt, the woman who answered the phone accused him of playing a cruel joke. For the man involved was her husband, and he had been dead for three years. Telly Savalas took the note round to her, and she agreed that the handwriting appeared to be that of her husband. She also said that the clothes the strange man wore seemed familiar. But how could the actor have received money from a ghost? This case is so odd and out of phase that I am tempted to argue that either it is a fairy-tale (or nice for an after-dinner speech) or the man had not really died and had just run away from his wife.

Still, I do have to beware of twisting the evidence if it does not seem to make much sense, so I will leave this one as it stands for now, simply pointing out that intervention into the real world by a ghost is very, very rare – which is one good reason why I feel entitled to my suspicions.

This collection of accounts is not given just to titillate. They serve to show the usual conditions under which a QC Experience takes place. All three were in the middle of the night, two in the bedroom and one on a lonely, deserted road in the midst of nowhere. The one thing they have in common is the lack of sensory stimulation.

From experiments which have been conducted, we know that if the brain stops receiving information from its normal sensory channels, it begins to get restless. It is customary for it to have to filter out an overload of data, and it abhors this dramatic decrease. So the brain soon tends to seek out new sources, and material from the subconscious and unconscious begins to come through. It is possible that a state like srm is reached, and species field information is relayed. These things tend to manifest as auditory or visual sensations – in other words, hallucinations. Generally speaking they are disorganized and a random jumble. But people who are prone to switching reality modes may find sensory deprivation a good way of precipitating a move into srm. Here more meaningful experiences can occur. Information which is obtained paranormally could be externalized as a much more coherent visionary phenomenon.

The Oz Factor symptoms which preface the onset of the QC Experience are interesting clues in this regard. The sudden disappearance of all ambient sounds and the strange isolation which the percipient claims (for instance, saying that a normally busy road was suddenly devoid of all traffic) point to a connection with sensory deprivation. It is as if the brain has to switch off the tap that allows the regular flow of sensory information to come in, so that it can switch on the tap which brings data from the deeper levels of consciousness.

The Oz Factor is a sort of induced sensory deprivation practised by the brain to allow entry into synchronistic reality mode. If you think about it, the act of meditation works in the same way. You quieten yourself down, even minimize your breathing in certain Yoga exercises, and so try to entice the brain into coming up with the Oz Factor to presage a QC Experience.

There is also a successful scientific experiment, known as the 'Ganzfeld', which is being used by research labs throughout the world, including that of parapsychologist Dr Carl Sargeant at Cambridge University. This involves techniques such as covers for the eyes and ears and the playing of white noise as the subject relaxes in a darkened room. Meanwhile, another person elsewhere tries to make use of the change in reality mode which this serves to induce by transmitting information through the medium of the mind. Again the core of the experiment seems to be sensory deprivation, attempting to coax the brain to produce the Oz Factor and lead the percipient into synchronistic reality mode.

That the bedroom is the place where many of these phenomena occur is already obvious from the stories in this book. It combines the advantages of sensory deprivation (no light or sound and constant, unchanging background) with the fact that the conscious mind is at a low ebb and has slid nearer to synchronistic reality mode where deeper level data can seep through. A whole range of phenomena known as 'bedroom visitors' results from this very situation. Here is a nice example.

It was 2.20 a.m. in an ordinary bedroom in an ordinary house in Manchester. A man and wife lay side by side, the wife asleep and the man, having read a book for several hours, now exhausted and ready to sleep himself. The room is dark and quiet as he lies back, his mind already lulled into the sort of state with which many of us are familiar when we read a book extensively. You can find yourself reading the same line over and over, or else going through a whole page without having really understood a single word. It is almost the same as a mild hypnotic trance.

The man in Manchester (whom we shall just call Len) suddenly discovers a chill running down his spine. Around the room is silence. But it is bright. There is a light like the moon filtering through the open curtains. Perhaps that indeed is exactly what it is. Convinced he is being foolish, he lies back to settle once again. But he is now expecting something to happen. When the cold sensation comes again, this time the Oz Factor seizes control. Of course, Len is not familiar with the Oz Factor. All he knows is that something very weird is taking place. As he put it later, 'I could not hear the clock ticking, and it was only about a foot away from me. Everything was – how should I explain it? – it was like everything had stood still.' His brain has shut off the tap that feeds in the normal sensory awareness. And it has opened up the one giving access to the deeper levels of mind. Desperate for a reason to explain what is happening, he externalizes the inflow of information. He sees a ghost.

At first Len imagines that the white figure coming towards him must be his young child. But the child is fast asleep elsewhere in the house. Then, as the figure reaches the end of the bed, it looks down at his wife. She too still sleeps by his side. It is only now that Len recognizes the face of the ghost. It is without any question the famous (but very dead) movie star Tyrone Power! 'I can swear to who it was,' Len was to admit. But at the time he just lay there, admiring the face, which was tanned, and the strange white clothes like a monk's habit which the 'ghost' was wearing. 'What's going on?' Len calls, and at this the figure turns around to stare at him, eyes glowing orange like car headlamps. It then starts to move in his direction! Desperately he shakes his wife, but she will not wake up. The image of Tyrone Power has now turned again and is heading out of the door. It seems perfectly solid and does not walk through the door or wall. There is little to distinguish it from the living body of the famous actor.

Eventually, when his wife does awaken, she has experienced nothing. Nor can she find a way to accept what Len keeps saying to her. But he calmly tells her, 'It was Tyrone Power I saw. I can swear to that, even if I die tonight.' For the next month after that, the light will remain on in his bedroom.

This is typical of the way a witness will go through a bedroom visitor experience. Most of the features which we see Len describing repeat in case after case. And again, as we often see, this is not a single isolated incident. A few weeks after Len decided to sleep in the dark once more, a strange 'man in black' appeared at the end of the bed. 'Not again!' he murmured. And at that it disappeared. The next morning he was the recipient of tragic news. His brother had died, and this was reported on a black-edged card.

Len's 'man in black' is easy to understand. Whilst in srm, his mind either detected bow-wave ripples from the reading of the postcard or harmonized with the mind of another of his relatives who knew that his brother was already dead. In either case the black figure was a pictorial expression of this weakly detected bit of information. The man for his brother, and the black as a symbol of death.

But what about Tyrone Power? Where could such a strange apparition emerge from? We do not know, but it is possible that his wife was dreaming about the movie star that night, perhaps even a sexual fantasy. It is certainly interesting that the 'ghost' was looking first at the sleeping woman. Here we may see an example of harmonic resonance between the minds of two people

who are very close, one asleep and in srm and the other awake in
that reality mode. In a sense Len came to share his wife's fantasy
and then project it into his own sphere of reality.

For actress Debbie Watling her recurrent bedroom visitor is
much more sinister. Indeed she has gone through repeated
encounters with what is often termed the 'night terror'. In such
cases the person feels a heavy pressure, and they may even find
themselves paralysed. In extreme cases a sexual liaison with an
invisible assailant is claimed. However, that is fairly unusual.
Most of the night terror reports are more run of the mill.

Certainly this experience is more common than people realize.
I often receive letters from frightened people who have
undergone strange buzzings or hummings whilst alone in their
bed, or felt a kind of electrical tingling sensation, or had the next
step in the phenomenon, the muscle paralysis. This can all occur
without anything else taking place. I know that when I was
young it was a regular thing for me to wake up in the night with
one or other of these symptoms. I also had a strange waking
experience, especially when I was in a stress situation. The only
way I can describe it is as if the atmosphere had suddenly turned
into transparent treacle soup! Everything seems to slow down
and the world echoes inside your head. It is a very nasty feeling. I
suspect that these are like training exercises in switching reality
modes. If you come through without too much fear, you slowly
learn to miss out these physiological stages and step from one
mode into another. If it scares you too much, they tend to be all
you ever experience of the paranormal.

A common by-product of this kind of thing is the viewing of
strange lights in the bedroom. This is more frequent when the
night terror happens during childhood. Nowadays we would
probably call these things UFOs, as young Gaynor Sunderland
from North Wales did. But they are more likely 'psychic toys'. In
other words, they are visualized external phenomena of the most
basic kind which can give useful tuition in how to control the QC
Experience. It is not without significance that Gaynor said these
lights often used to 'come and play'. Eventually she went on to
toy with more elaborate visualizations, including aliens Arna and
Parz (see my book *Alien Contact*). But she grew out of these ('I
don't need them any more,' she told me one day). By the time she
was a teenager (and she is still only that as I write), her psychic
abilities were being channelled in other directions of a more

conventional kind. (See, for instance, *The Green Stone*.) I doubt if we have heard the last of this young lady.

Debbie Watling had lights coming to play in her childhood bedroom too. These would often announce an attack by the night terror. The next step was, as she put it, 'everything goes terribly silent.' This is the Oz Factor taking hold. Eventually she reached the stage of the pressure from above and total paralysis. This may simply be the brain interpreting its order to stop the inflow of normal sensory information a bit too literally. It is the ultimate sensory deprivation trick! Debbie became scared and found she could stop the phenomenon at this point by reciting the Lord's Prayer. Doubtless this works by focusing and concentrating the mind, bringing it back into normal reality mode.

You might regard these terminated phenomena as an aborted Quasi-Conscious Experience. The fear prevents any paranormal happenings from taking place. But at times Debbie has gone past this stage and undergone visualizations, and it is these which act as the source for her belief in the demonic origin of the night terror, explaining why she recites a prayer to ward it off. She has 'seen' a half goat/man creature bending over her bed. She even says she has reached out and touched it. It does seem that her devilish interpretation of the QC Experience has transmitted itself to her ability visually to externalize what she senses about it. It is a shame that she did not have more pleasant dreams when a child, at the point when she probably first created this gruesome monster to take the blame for what was occurring. If she had used alien imagery, like Gaynor Sunderland, it might have been less psychologically trying.

Hollywood loves this sort of horror-fiction stuff. And claims of rape by spacemen, demons or spooks are prime fodder for a movie or two. We have already seen *The Exorcist*, *The Omen* and their endless sequels. And the film *The Entity* concerns a sexually aggressive night terror which attacked a young American woman. It is based on the book of this name, which stems (allegedly) from the files of a real psychiatrist about one of his strangest cases. But it is not that strange. Anomaly researchers could list dozens of examples.

This Hollywood fad for hyping up fact with dramatic special effects and liberal doses of 'fictionalization' reached its heights (or depths) of absurdity in the saga of *The Amityville Horror*, told in the film of that name and in its imitations (the third Amityville story even being in shock-inducing 3-D!). In these movies the poor viewer, paranormal researcher or member of the public faced impossible odds when trying to decide if something was fact, fiction or that new invention 'faction' (a cross between the two). It is doubtful if the producers were sure themselves half the time. They might even have been responsible for fixing a norm within the species field. If so, when you consider some of the dreadful scenes they had to offer (oozing slime, devil's footprints and bloodbaths), they may have a lot to answer for. By not calling it all fiction from the start, they enhanced its impact, which was of course the whole point. But this must have increased the effect on the species field.

There *are* some true facts about the Amityville story, you may be surprised to learn. These were first told in a book by Jay Anson (noted for his work on horror *fiction*). The large rambling house on Ocean Avenue, Long Island, New York, *was* the home of convicted killer Ronald de Feo, who on 13 November 1974 went crazy and shot to death his mother, father, brothers and sisters as all six lay in bed. De Feo claimed insanity and the hearing of voices (a not uncommon plea in such cases), but this was all rejected by the courts and he was sentenced to six consecutive life terms in prison.

On 18 December 1975 a young couple with three children and a few money problems (which may or may not have been relevant) moved in, having bought the house at a bargain price because of its year-long lack of occupants and terrible history. They stayed just four weeks, and it is during this crucial time that all of what did or did not happen is said to have occurred.

In their original local press interviews soon after the events, the family claimed only fairly mild experiences – the feeling of a presence, doors and windows opening on their own, and so forth. Interesting stuff, but nothing that would distinguish it from thousands of hauntings or small-scale poltergeist cases. Their departure from the house appears to have had as much to do with their inability to afford its running costs as anything else. But then Ronald de Feo's defence lawyer, William Weber, seems to have had quite an idea. If he could promote the story that the house was haunted, he might be able to get his client off on remarkable grounds. So he arranged for prime time on television and radio for the house's latest occupants to describe their month of terror. And they were pushed onwards towards the inevitable book (subtitled 'A True Story', by Jay Anson) and then the movie, starring James Brolin, Margot Kidder and Rod Steiger. In the course of this long process the truth, shall we say, became a little blurred. There is quite a gulf between the original press claims and those recounted in the book and film. Here we now find levitations, exorcisms, phantom voices and green slimes. However, in a 1979 press statement, Weber admitted, 'We created this horror story over many bottles of wine.' This does tend to indicate the true reality status of the Amityville horror.

Scant attention seems to have been paid towards the real facts by those involved in the later embellishments. At least, if you look at the reports made by several paranormal research groups after the family had first left the house, you begin to get suspicions. For example, Dr Stephen Kaplan, a parapsychologist, said, 'It is our professional opinion that the story of this haunting is mostly fiction.' The Psychical Research Foundation, who were quickly onto the scene, say they dropped the case after preliminary study because the claims of the family were atypical of that kind of experience and were supported by almost no evidence.

One of the best investigations, published after the book but before the movie, was by Peter Jordan and Rick Moran. They checked into everything and everybody. Local repairmen said they had not fixed the gross damage to the house, as claimed. Local police insisted they had not inspected the house, as alleged. The priest shown in the film as conducting an exorcism in the bedroom was adamant he had not been inside the house, let alone been evicted by a spectral voice or given a mysterious skin disease by the demons in possession of the building. His colleague, who was in the car with him when according to the book an evil power took it over and led to a dreadful crash, says they just got a flat tyre! And so it goes on.

It would seem that whoever was responsible, and for whatever reason, a concerted effort was made to jazz up a pretty mundane tale. By calling it 'one of the most terrifying true cases ever', its success was assured. You might say, so what? If they made money out of a hoax, what does it matter if people enjoyed it? But in the world of strange phenomena the borderline between hoax and truth, fact and fiction, is hazy to start with. It is potentially dangerous to affect the species field in such a big way by creating untruths of such a nasty nature, aside from the difficulties it brings to anyone seeking to make these phenomena respectable to science.

Sadder still is the fact that the house in Amityville may well have had an aura of some sort associated with it. You would expect some ripples to be left by the emotional and physical carnage that went on in there. The building could act like an object at the focus of a psychometry experience.

In Britain, the house at Hattersley on the edge of the Pennines once occupied by the multiple child-murderers Myra Hindley and Ian Brady also seems to have a residual energy of some kind. There have been repeated stories since the dastardly deeds of 1966 that nobody will stay there for very long because of its 'bad vibes'. 'Bad vibrations' may indeed not be too far removed from the truth. After all, that is only what Susannah York claims to have experienced.

Movies about the paranormal are certainly big business, and likely to remain so as long as man is tantalized by things he does not understand. Sometimes they are created because of the dreams or real adventures of their makers. Steven Spielberg's *Poltergeist* has an origin in a childhood bedroom visitor phenomenon he went through. At other times the movies seem to precipitate events themselves. *Close Encounters of the Third Kind* involved some UFO sightings by many of those who took part in its making.

In fact 1977, the year *Close Encounters* burst upon the public, may well be regarded as the zenith of our society's love affair with the paranormal. Not only did it see the biggest wave of UFO sightings ever to take place, certainly in Britain, but the biggest international success of all time, when the movie *Star Wars*, was released by George Lucas.

In this space-age fairy-tale Lucas first markets his marvellous concept of *the* basic principle of the universe. It has entered our vocabulary through the phrase 'May the force be with you.' Lucas says himself of his creation, 'the Force', that it is 'the energy field that all living things generate', which makes it sound rather familiar to us. Actor Alec Guinness, who played the Jedi Knight who uses 'the Force' for good, in his battles against the renegade knight 'Darth Vader', says he was inundated with letters from people who seemed to believe in the reality of the phenomenon. 'I thought it was supposed to be fiction,' he claimed. Little did he know!

With this idea Lucas has come closer than any other movie man to capturing what is probably the real essence of the cosmos. 'The Force' is a fine name indeed for the life field, not only of the species but more likely of the whole sentient universe. It is the universal consciousness of which we all form a part. By his image of a suitably trained knight tuning into it and then using it to shape reality (creating psychokinetic effects for example), he graphically dramatizes what we have discussed in this book. And we discovered that not from the fantasies of outer space but from the realities of life on earth.

'The Force' can be used for good or for evil. It can change reality for the better or the worse. It can lead to your prescribing behaviour that will create a happy situation or to destructive poltergeist phenomena. It really all depends on you.

I had a fascinating dream during the night after I wrote the above, causing me to change the ending of this chapter. In this I could feel 'the Force'. I was able to move objects just by thinking about it. I often used to have a dream like that in childhood and recall the delight it gave me then. This new dream recaptured a little of that bliss at being able to do such impossible things.

I found myself at the end of a room (one I used to live in as a child – which emphasizes that this is a faculty adults *lose*). My mother was seated in a chair at the other end, and I was mentally picking up objects and floating them around the room in front of her. 'She knows it can't be me,' I kept thinking, as I watched in amusement her puzzled looks. Then I picked up a bowl of sugar with my mind and tipped its contents over her head! My laughter was short-lived. I began to feel great embarrassment and shame. All I could think to myself was, 'Why am I using this power for such stupid purposes? Why don't I do something useful?' So I levitated myself instead of the sugar bowl and flew through the roof as if it wasn't there. The last thing I recall is heading off in the general direction of the stars.

This was a beautiful dream, full of emotion, and it makes the excellent point that your consciousness can often wrestle with a problem and then express it much better with its symbols and images whilst in synchronistic reality mode. The many phenomena that we experience in this strange world are in themselves neither good nor bad: they are what we choose to make of them. We have the ability to prescript the future and make the world a better place. We could stop all our spending on technology reaching ever upwards to the sky (for exploratory and destructive purposes) and use the money to cure poverty instead. For we will never reach the stars in a rocket ship, but we may get there with our minds.

There is only one thing stopping such miracles from happening. And *we* are that one thing.

In *Star Wars* 'Luke Skywalker' has to make an attack in his spacecraft whilst it has a faulty computer. The aim is so difficult that a strike looks impossible. But suddenly he senses a voice in his mind. It is that of the Jedi Knight who taught him to use 'The Force', 'Obi Wan Ben Kenobi'. Kenobi had been slain by Darth Vader but at death his body had vanished. Luke does not know if the voice he hears is his own inner self using the image of his teacher to push him in the right direction, or if some aspect of Kenobi's spirit has somehow survived. This is exactly the dilemma we also face. 'Use the force, Luke,' the voice tells him. He does and the battle is won. Technology is no match for the correct application of the mind.

Our challenges and our choices are very similar to those Luke Skywalker faced. But wherever the voice comes from, and whatever the truth about the visions which we see, the solution to the many grave crises on this earth probably lies in some simple words. When Obi Wan Ben Kenobi was instructing Luke in how to control reality and win his victories over chance, he advised him very quietly: 'Feel The Force – and let it direct you.' I wouldn't argue with that as a philosophy of life.

11. Stars and the After-life

'An awful lot of people are afraid to believe that death is *not* the end' – Lee Everett (medium).

I have only ever been to one seance, and it was not what I expected. There were no darkened rooms or trappings of ectoplasm, no visits from Indian guides or great Chinese prophets. It was at a rather ordinary village hall in the beautiful Staffordshire countryside, with full lights blazing and the medium a rather personable middle-aged lady. She sat there chatting away to those of us present, as if we had come round for a cup of tea. Occasionally she would relay information which she said had been obtained from the 'other side'. Her references to aunts and uncles and others now deceased were pretty matter of fact. Yet their origin was supposed to be a land beyond death, a place towards which we are all travelling. Then she announced that a horse had just entered the hall. She said it so naturally that I instinctively looked around to view this curious sight. Of course, there was no such beast. At least not in normal, everyday reality. Yet, as she went on to describe in great detail what was clearly visible to her, it was obvious that the horse did exist in some sort of reality, somewhere.

We never did discover what that horse was supposed to represent, although it was apparently a former pet of somebody in the room. However, this little episode did open up my mind to the question of survival. I was, and still am, undecided as to whether this is fact or self-inflicted fantasy. But I have to admit that to this medium, and all others like her, death is just life in a different dimension. It is one of the most natural things in the world.

The question of whether or not some aspect of ourselves survives the dissolution of the body is perhaps the greatest single enigma which mankind confronts. We may evade and put off considering it. We might try to run from it down the apparently different (yet rather similar) roads of blind atheism and religion. But one thing is sure: it gets every one of us in the end. One day in that great mysterious void we call the future there will come a point where our physical bodies cease to function (either by wearing out, becoming diseased or just breaking up in an accident). It matters not if you are unknown or a celebrity: death claims us all in time.

We have already met some tales of famous ghosts. Here is another one.

Rudolph Messner is considered by many who know the subject to be the greatest mountaineer who ever lived. He enjoys climbing alone and has challenged more giant peaks than anyone else. Often he has undergone strange experiences. He has floated out of his body, has found himself in telepathic communication with others when he has climbed with someone, and has several times been accompanied by a spook!

Perhaps the most interesting occasion is when Messner chose to make a daring solo ascent of Mount Everest without oxygen equipment. He was followed on this climb by the ghost of the British explorer George Leigh Mallory, who never returned from his attempt to conquer the peak in 1924. Messner had a couple of visual apparitions of the dead man, who allegedly pointed out the spot (officially unknown) where he met his doom. Was it an hallucination brought on by the solitude and rarefied atmosphere, he wonders. He feels dubious of that. Messner seems to believe that he encountered the spirit or life field of the great mountaineer who is 'still there [on the side of Everest] . . . in another "kind of life" '.

Of course, it is true that lack of oxygen in high mountains can create changes in blood chemistry and produce hallucinations. The same is true of some drugs. And the process of sensory deprivation (such as can occur with great physical endurance for long periods in a desolate environment) has demonstrably generated the same thing. But then again I am not denying that ghosts *are* a kind of hallucination. They are the results of subjective information gained in synchronistic reality mode being overdubbed onto the 'real' world of normal reality mode. Messner probably attuned himself to information out of the species field and then used this as the source of a visual drama representing Mallory.

Similar things have been reported by long-distance solo yachtsmen and rowers such as Sir Francis Chichester, Thor Heyerdahl and John Ridgeway. Their visual hallucinations, doubtless produced in such a fashion, include UFOs emerging from the ocean, sea-serpents and the ghost of a crewman out of a Christopher Columbus voyage, who guided the modern sailor through a storm! These were not hallucinations in the sense of being distorted or vague. They looked totally real and were doubtless QC Experiences.

What is a medium? This is the word we use to describe a person who claims to be in regular contact with the dead. They see and hear 'spirits' often. But how do we know that they are just not undergoing strong and persistent visual and auditory hallucinations? The truth is that we do not know. Indeed, there is evidence to suggest that psychologically these people tend to have excellent powers of imagery. The case of 'Ruth', reported by psychiatrist Dr Morton Schatzman, is perhaps the best example. She was eventually able to control the various talking spectres she observed, and often they were of living people who were probably elsewhere at the time! Scientific experiments showed that the whole environment (background *and* apparition) was hallucinated and over-dubbed onto reality. So this could easily be true of a medium.

Mediums may just be very gifted at switching reality modes. The difference between them and the person who has regular 'psychic' experiences, or just the very rare one-off occurrence, may well be no more than degree.

But there have been fake mediums too. That fact, undenied by paranormal researchers, probably accounts for the lack of credibility afforded this question, for if one medium can prey on the desire of the bereaved to get in touch with their dead, surely it is possible that they all might.

This was the basic philosophy of Harry Houdini, the great magician and escapologist, who began a crusade against the phoneys of Spiritualism. There are paranormal researchers willing to believe that Houdini was himself psychic. They could see no explanation for some of his feats, such as exploding cabinets, staying underwater without breathing for an hour or more, and apparently obtaining information by telepathy or precognition. Even fellow artists said his often glib solutions for these things were impossible. And there were occasions when the great showman himself admitted that he had no real explanation for what he did. He just did it!

Houdini was absolutely certain that no medium *could* be genuine, and he often went to very elaborate lengths to prove his point. There is sufficient prima-facie evidence to suggest that, when he came across a medium allegedly obtaining information from a 'spirit' which he could not disprove by normal means, he planted or fabricated false evidence to try to succeed where science had failed.

Houdini's war against the psychics was undoubtedly a heated one, and he ensured that controversy trailed in his wake. What motivated him to fight with such tenacity remains obscure, but it does seem to be a legacy he has handed down to other magicians. There is practically a war between the members of the Magic Circle and those who profess to be mediums or psychic. Even today public unmaskings go on.

Uri Geller, who began as a nightclub magician but became an international superstar, claiming his powers were paranormal, has been the subject of vitriolic attacks. The evidence appears to suggest that he has abilities but has never been opposed to enhancing them with tricks and bravado whenever he felt them necessary or appropriate. Scientists have in the main come down in his favour. Magicians, taking on Houdini's mantle, have been scathing.

In the USA, one magician named James 'The Amazing' Randi has done all he can to expose each and every medium he can find. He has seeded false clients into their midst, led them into traps and duplicated the 'tricks' which they purport to do by powers of the mind. He and a vigilante squad known as CSICOP (Committee for the Scientific Investigation of Claims of the Paranormal) have been formed to fight 'pseudoscience', which is their word for things such as UFOs, ghosts and psychics.

The British equivalent of Randi, although less vociferous, is Paul Daniels, who is now a media star with his own TV spectaculars. His views about mediums and strange phenomena are often made crystal clear, and he has duplicated tricks to try to show how spirit voices and messages can originate. 'Under laboratory conditions' is another misleading favourite item on his television show. Here he conducts a 'psychic' experiment with a TV camera looking down from directly overhead and claims to do exactly what a psychic can, but with trickery. On no occasion that I have seen him do this has he *ever* attempted more than a few card tricks. He has not effected random-number generators or gone out of the body. Often it takes little skill, just sharp eyesight, to spot the way he persuades the audience to be fooled.

Paul Daniels, like most magicians, runs scared in the face of psychics. Magicians see them as a threat to their livelihood, because you do not need to be a member of the Magic Circle to outdo their tricks. All of us are potential psychics.

There are indeed *real* mediums – people who are, at the very least, remarkably gifted in the arts of perception. It is likely, in my opinion, that they do possess ability to switch reality modes and can in that state pick up information from what we might otherwise call paranormal sources. Whether these sources have anything to do with life after death is a different question altogether and much less easy to decide.

Doris Stokes is one of the most famous mediums in the world today. She is a large, gregarious and marvellously charismatic lady. At her performances (for there is no better word to describe them) she is immaculately dressed and talks to the often overflowing crowds with the ordinary manner of a housewife. Following her first autobiography, *Voices in my Ear* (1980), she has published several other volumes describing her life history and amazing claims. Each has been a smash-hit best seller. But she is less interested in money than in trying to prove her case that we do survive death.

Her messages are received, as her book title suggests, in the form of voices inside her inner ear. They are real in only a subjective sense because nobody else hears them, but they do seem to pass on information and allegedly have all the characteristics of coming from the once living, now dead, individual. If you study her sessions (and she cares not if there are millions watching via television or just a handful in a private room), you will find yourself at the same time frustrated and baffled. You will be frustrated because she often looks as if she is groping around, fishing through a sea of discarnate entities clamouring for her attention. Names pop out and apparently mean little. It all looks like a sham. But then suddenly she makes her mark. A name brings instant recognition. As she and that anxious, excited relative atune to one another, a torrent of information begins to flood out. From the name 'Tom' she builds up to saying things like, 'He died recently, didn't he, love?' and then, 'Yes. He's only been there a year or so. He says remember the red rose.' And so on. All this makes sense to the recipient of the message – at least so they claim. And not only that person, but most of the rest of the audience are entranced from that point on.

We shall not be surprised to learn that Doris was noted for her psychic abilities even as a child. She seems to have been born with the gift of switching reality modes with a facility beyond that we could even afford regular psychics, such as Lindsay Wagner. It might not be unlike musical ability, for example. Some of us are born with a lot, others with none at all. By training, a very few of those with a lot can become musical geniuses, and a little can be taught to those who previously had none.

Doris, as we might anticipate, could manifest her abilities whilst in srm by a variety of different methods. For instance, she once visually externalized the 'ghost' of her dead father, who informed her that, despite all the evidence to the contrary, her husband had *not* been killed overseas (it was war-time). 'I never lied to you, did I, doll?' he is supposed to have said. And all the information 'he' gave her turned out to be correct. Her husband was alive. Yet had she obtained this by way of bow-wave ripples of her eventual discovery of the news?

Mediums like Doris (and there are several others equally gifted) have a very similar life pattern. Usually they demonstrate a range of guises whilst in srm. They have seen UFOs or had bedroom encounters with fairy-like creatures. They have suffered poltergeist outbreaks or have channelled this same energy to cure sick animals. They have undergone OOBEs or have detected bow-wave ripples from major future events. And so on. There is little doubt in my mind that many of the people paranormal researchers meet who have frequent strange experiences of these kinds (and if you have one, you tend to have them all) have potential to be trained *into* mediums. A medium is nothing more than somebody who has decided to go in this particular direction as a habit pattern once they enter srm. They could have chosen to go in a quite different direction altogether, having OOBEs all the time, for example, or regularly encountering UFOs. The manner of use of their ability to switch modes is really up to them.

Matthew Manning is one of the rare male mediums (they are much more often women, as indeed are abductees by UFOs, two facts that are signficant and clearly not unrelated). Manning first encountered poltergeist and apparitional phenomena in adolescence and then began to develop his abilities through automatic writing and painting (see p. 137). Being a very intelligent young man, he became eager to learn the scientific basis of the amazing things he knew he could do, so he spent a lot of time in his early twenties touring laboratories around the world doing experiments with scientists. In the process he found himself using his skills on things like metal-bending and other demonstrations of psychokinesis – phenomena he would not have performed spontaneously but which he could do with ease when he applied himself that way. Finally he decided to stop 'playing' and instead put his efforts into healing.

All of this seems to be the same basic capacity to do things. But it is up to the individual how he channels it at any one point in time. Recall what was said in the last chapter about George Lucas and 'The Force'.

Doris Stokes frankly admits that sometimes, when for no accountable reason the voices just stop, she is tempted to cheat and occasionally has made up messages. The fact that they are accepted as readily as her 'real' ones is an important point. In fairness there is no good reason why most of what these mediums come up with cannot be explained as a further example of externalizing an *internal* process to deny responsibility. The spirit voices of Doris Stokes may be the equivalent of spacemen in UFO encounters, or Uri Geller's computer. Being so gifted at switching reality modes, she can pick up the life fields of all those living people who surround her during performances. They will be thinking of their deceased relatives and she could 'fish out tiddlers' of information and by a process of confabulation concoct and offer a relevant 'message'.

Are there any mediums who are famous in some other sphere of life? Indeed there are. There is every reason to suggest that someone like Lindsay Wagner qualifies for that term, and somebody who certainly does is former 'Goon' and television comic Michael Bentine.

Bentine's interest and involvement in the paranormal have been known to his colleagues and researchers in this field for many years. in 1975 he and I did a late-night radio show in which I discussed UFOs and he chatted about his work in the entertainments field. Between records I had a fascinating talk with this lovely man about his secret life, which has been chock full of strange phenomena. He told me about a UFO close encounter which he underwent many years ago in India and that he was perfectly satisfied that what he witnessed that day was no ordinary, earthly object. Some years later he was willing to endorse that view in public when he appeared on the TV show *The Sky at Night* when it debated UFOs. Michael put forward the case that UFOs *were* real but surprisingly did not describe his own sighting. The counter-argument that there was no evidence for UFOs came from that versatile television performer Patrick Moore.

Patrick must be one of the favourites of any mimic, with his delightfully original personality. In his books and public performances he is highly critical about UFOs to the point of extremity. Once he told some witnesses to a very spectacular long-duration UFO (which nobody else in a city of a million inhabitants on a sunny summer evening had seen) that they had just watched a pretty meteor! That idea is so silly that I am tempted to conclude he was joking. But when I once challenged him about his attitude to the phenomenon, he answered in simple graphic terms. On top of his gigantic 'P M' signature he wrote 'UFOs' are absolute rot!'

But Michael Bentine stood up to him bravely and even got Patrick to admit that he had once investigated a local UFO sighting which had truly baffled him. I have several very good reasons for thinking that, as with a lot of people, the private opinions of Patrick Moore bear little resemblance to those he seems willing to venture out in the open.

Sighting UFOs is by no means the only evidence that Michael Bentine enters synchronistic reality mode very often. He has recently chosen to tell the world of his other adventures in the realms of the mysterious, through his book *The Door Marked Summer*, one of the most pleasing reads within the literature of the paranormal. Michael's experiences range far and wide, over premonitions and telepathic communications. The Oz Factor symptoms are frequently related, and he has clearly undergone many QC Experiences. When he tragically lost his son in an air crash, he found himself receiving messages from him, assuring him that all was well and that there was a continuing life after bodily death. It is a very moving and sincerely related story. Bentine offered an address to ASSAP when the association was launched in London in October 1981 and is now one of the best assets the subject has from a vast range of entertainers who are supporters of our psychic lives.

Michael Bentine and Doris Stokes are mediums of the type known as 'clairaudient': they hear voices from the 'other side'. Others are clairvoyant: they see pictures or visions. But Lee Everett is very different. She is a transfiguration medium.

Lee is the former wife of Kenny Everett, a radio and television star with a zany sense of humour. But he never had a laugh at the expense of Lee. She was the typical developing medium, moving through sporadic premonitions onto the ability to perform healing. Finally, at age thirty-seven, she began her strange attempts at transfiguration. She works alongside a clairaudient, who first picks up a voice and then transmits a brief message to the person in the audience for whom this is meant. Lee then notices her face begin to change shape and take on a passable imitation of the communicator of the message, even in situations where that communicator is a man! Mind you, Lee admits that, if someone complains that the spirit had a beard in real life, there is nothing she can do about that! As Lee tells us about what happens to her in such transfigurations, it is evident she has entered synchronistic reality mode. She loses all control of her own body, and it moulds itself like plasticine.

Of course, this sounds quite incredible – one might be tempted to say impossible – but it seems to be a growing form of mediumship these days. Lee does not work in the same bright conditions as Doris Stokes, and photographs of transfigurations are few and of limited quality. It is said that the process is very difficult, which may be true. Perhaps one day a medium will become adept enough to do it anywhere, and we shall get some probative film. Until then, as usual, we are left merely tantalized.

Now you might find this both convenient and suspicious – indeed it may well be. However, even if transfiguration were proved to occur, it would be only another step along the road towards proof. It would not itself be proof of survival. There is every reason to suppose that the facial muscles of a person could be controlled by the mind of that person, to take on the pictorial reflection of somebody she 'sees' in her imagination. In cases of extreme hysteria, or under hypnosis, there is already good evidence that mind can shape matter. Stigmata marks or psychosomatic weals have all been produced, even apparent evidence of lash marks on the back, all simply by the mind of the person concerned. And medical records contain some fascinating cases of miracle cures from disfiguring illnesses where skin ailments have disappeared just by thinking long and hard enough.

Obviously there must be limits to this sort of phenomenon, but it seems quite feasible that distorting the shape of the face a bit (which we can all do to an extent in any case) is realistic, especially when it need not be too exact. We all have the psychological quirk of seeing faces in the fire. If someone is convinced the medium is physically adapting himself to look like a dead relative, they will likely accept a much poorer representation of that loved one than under ordinary circumstances.

So, even the extraordinary phenomenon of transfiguration cannot allow us to choose between real communication from the dead and internally generated paranormal messages. To be sure, it does make life tougher for the proponent of the 'inner source' theory. In Lee Everett's case we have to accept that her clairaudient companion first detects the information and externalizes it as a voice and message. He then had somehow to transmit this to Lee, or she has to tune into the same set of information, before coming up with a visual image of the dead communicant and subconsciously using this to mould her face. This is not impossible, but it presumes a lot.

The ouija board has all the letters of the alphabet on its friction-reduced surface. A group of people sit with fingers lightly touching a pointer, trying not to move it but concentrating on making contact with a dead spirit. Eventually the pointer does move and seems to spell out meaningful messages (although just as often it spells out utter gibberish!). This probably reflects the jumbled content of the subconscious minds of those present, and usually of the one most dominant. It is fairly easy to concentrate on a certain letter and 'force' the pointer there even when you can be sure you have not physically moved it. That probably stems from faint muscle actions on the threshold of awareness.

Many years ago, when I was working in an office during college holidays, I used to experiment with the ouija board with some of the girls during our lunch break. My interest in the paranormal was just beginning, and I was very naïve then. I distinctly recall perfecting the technique discussed above and, although I was now convinced there was nothing in the board of real interest to me, playing a trick on my workmates. I made the board spell out a message from an address in Aberdeen where the 'spirit' was advising us he had left some buried treasure when he died. So convincing was this that it proved hard for me to tell the truth. There was much excitement, and I have to admit I was almost persuaded onto the next train to Scotland!

Matthew Manning began automatic writing when still at school. Often masses of this appeared on his bedroom wall and was signed by many famous folk, in particular the owner of the house years before, who eventually became a 'friendly ghost' whom Matthew met often. It ought not to astonish you that automatic production of more creative material is also common. Indeed, Manning went on to some spectacular examples himself.

This creative material includes literature (novels dictated from the beyond), music and art. We have seen how artistic/creative people are the sort most often associated with srm, so it hardly seems coincidence that it is the same processes which manifest themselves most strongly when they are produced through a medium.

We have already noted how many famous novelists felt that their work 'wrote itself'. They were doubtless performing a mild form of automatic writing. This seems to blend towards the other extreme demonstrated by Mrs Curran, an American who, after using an ouija board, began to receive not just messages but whole novels from a character named 'Patience Worth'. She said that she had been born in England and moved to the USA where she was killed by Indians in the century before she began dictations to her 'literary agent'. These dictations were historical novels spanning many different eras and were well received by the critics. Yet there is no evidence that Patience Worth is a real person and not just an externalized *alter ego* of Mrs Curran. Joan Grant has written novels in a similar way, but she claims them to be the histories of her own 'past lives', although her memories of these are so extensive and detailed that they seem hard to accept as this.

What is the difference between Charles Dickens or Robert Louis Stevenson having a totally fictitious novel dedicated by their subconscious, the 'ghost' of Patience Worth writing novels through Mrs Curran, and the 'past lives' of Joan Grant transmitting themselves to be turned into novels? The answer may well be precious little. Each of these phenomena is just a different way of expressing the same process of internal data flow. In the first case the true source is accepted. In the last it is accepted but regarded as different 'lives' of the self, instead of different internal levels of the self. And in the case of Mrs Curran total transfer of the problem onto an external source takes place. At least, on the basis of the evidence as we have it so far, that seems to be the way of it.

Matthew Manning is one of a rare breed of 'psychic artists', and his repertoire is amazing. He just sits down and lets his hand do its own thing. Eventually, with no direction on his part, he claims, a painting will be completed that is plainly in the style of a famous dead artist. It may be a copy of a previous work or a new one altogether. Often his paintings are signed. Whilst Manning is very cautious about what he believes concerning these pictures, he does say that when a particular artist is painting through him he feels an individual character as if it is a real person. Picasso, for example, who has offered several 'works', can be very violent and energy-draining.

Rosemary Brown is a remarkable London housewife with a lot in common with Matthew Manning. Again her psychic talents were obvious in childhood, and again they appeared in many different guises. She had a visual apparition when just aged seven of a man she later came to recognize as the classical musician Franz Liszt. He told her that he was going to make her a famous musician. By the time she was an adult, this seemed like a wild prediction, for she had struggled to learn the piano but given up after a year. Her tutor told her she had no real talent. Then, in 1964, with Rosemary now a widow, Liszt returned, and along with him came a stream of composers from Beethoven, Bach and Chopin to Stravinsky. They visually appear to her, looking like ordinary people (which, as you will know by now, is very much the rule for a 'ghost'). Mrs Brown talks happily to them and to whoever else is 'really' in the room with her, and takes down like a stenographer fully composed new pieces of music which they offer. She goes so fast that it is hard to believe she is faking, and there is no real doubt about her ability as she is happy to perform in front of television cameras.

What of the music? Beethoven has produced parts of his 10th and 11th Symphonies. Schubert has given a mammoth sonata. And there are hundreds more. (As with Matthew Manning, Mrs Brown insists that each composer has a unique style and character. Sometimes they lapse into their native tongue if she is slow to understand, and she says she has to write down their words and have them translated later.) Most of the compositions are well beyond the ordinary musical ability of Rosemary Brown to play, let alone compose. Some of it has been recorded, and even the biggest sceptic has agreed that if it is fakery it is pretty good. Many others are satisfied that no woman with or without musical talent could possibly produce such a rich variety of classical material from over twenty different world famous composers, always maintaining at least a reasonable standard.

Mrs Brown also does a little psychic art (including paintings by van Gogh and Debussy, who has taken to paints instead of musical notes, it seems!), and she believes she has had conversations with other famous dead people, including Albert Einstein and Bertrand Russell.

All of these artistic and musical creations are fascinating stuff, but is it just the natural talent of the individual being stretched beyond normal limits, in the same way as synchronistic reality mode can produce novels and solutions to problems? We can probably just about accept that, although it is hard to conceive why Rosemary Brown should always feel the need not just to visualize but to hold long and supposedly meaningful conversations with figments of her imagination.

It is also very intriguing that these artists and musicians are always dead. We have seen that apparitions of living people can be visualized, so we might wonder if it would be possible to obtain songs, poems, books or paintings from contemporary, living, famous people. It would be interesting to see if Rosemary Brown could provide us with a new Paul McCartney melody, for example. But researchers into the paranormal often run away from ideas like that, because they want to believe that cases such as those discussed in this chapter prove life after death, when they may prove only that our life before death is a whole lot richer than we realize.

It also worries me that, if Rosemary Brown can talk to Albert Einstein, why has he failed to give us something useful? Assuming he has had a few years in the after-life to carry on working, we might expect him, or some other genius who has been dead for even longer, to have promoted a major scientific breakthrough by now. A cure for cancer would not be a bad start. That we keep getting nothing more provocative or valuable that Beethoven's 11th Symphony seems to pose a few questions that deserve answers.

Leslie Flint is a medium of the kind known as a 'direct voice'. He actually reproduces the voice of the dead person. This can occur even if his mouth is blocked up with sticking tape or otherwise securely gagged. Journalist Bob Chapman of the science department at the *Sunday Express* has carried out tests into his authenticity and pronounced his abilities genuine. Even with a throat microphone to rule out the option of clever ventriloquism, the voices kept on appearing.

A galaxy of dead stars manifested during Leslie Flint's long career. By strange irony the idol of the silent screen, Rudolph Valentino, was one of his most prolific guides, speaking often and appearing as an apparition dressed like a sheikh (one of his most famous movie roles). The messages which an obviously sincere Flint had to offer are not exactly earth-shattering. Marilyn Monroe did want to clear up the mystery of her death: the drug overdose which killed her was not suicide but an accident. But for Oscar Wilde to complain that he was not getting any royalties from his after-death success, and for flying ace Amy Johnson to bemoan the lack of aircraft on the other side, all seems just a little bit facetious. But then who knows? Wilde was noted for his wry humour. And perhaps there are no aerial transports on the astral plane.

Can we make any sense out of all these ideas and possibilities? Are we any nearer to answering that ultimate question about life and death? It is something which we would all dearly like to know. Our existence would be so much more secure and comfortable if we did not have that awful instant trapdoor to the dark pit of infinity waiting ahead of us. Or maybe that very security would produce careless human beings without due consideration for the sanctity of life?

I am not sure the price of total conviction of life after death would be worth paying. Not if that price was wholesale murder and violence, on the pretext that it hardly mattered since nobody actually died. Can we trust human nature sufficiently to say that this is pessimistic nonsense?

Still, let us examine a possible scenario, based upon the concepts of the life field and its potential existence after death.

. What happens then to our life field or consciousness? Does it simply fade away like a morning mist evaporated by the rays of the sun? Or does it somehow remain vibrant and alive in a manner which we can only guess at? It is to that ultimate question which we now find ourselves drawn as we approach the end of our quest.

If all that we have met so far is akin to fundamental reality, or the way that things truly *do* happen, it is at least possible that something survives. It does look as if mind is not just a consequence of greater and greater complexity within the brain. Consciousness appears to evolve in parallel with the physical matter of which brain is just a remarkable creation. Our mind is grander than that of the ant, but both do have consciousness. Indeed, everything may well have consciousness of some sort.

Mind uses brain, rather as electromagnetic energy uses a television set to produce sound and pictures. If we ask what that picture is, there are few of us (however lacking in knowledge about the workings of TV sets) who would argue that the picture is *inside* the set. Yet smash the set, or let it run on and on until it wears out, and what happens? The picture disappears. Of course, we realize that the energy which is truly the picture is there all the time. The set merely brings it into our reality. It allows us to detect it because our bodies are not equipped to sense raw electromagnetic energy. If we plug in a new set or fix the old one, the picture magically comes back to life.

Our brains and our bodies are probably the equivalent of the electronic wizardry which the television represents. Sometimes our doctors, like TV repairmen, can fix us up and bring us back to life. At other times our physical structure is too far gone. We are dead. But if our consciousness is truly like the electromagnetic energy which flows through the TV set, even at death it is still there. Its essential reality is independent of the brain and the body. It can exist without it, although, for it to manifest in our world, our normal everyday reality, it has to interact with our brains in order to produce a picture.

Our sense of 'I', of being here, is just the picture on the TV screen. Our real sense of being, our consciousness, is the signal behind the scenes which allows the miracle to happen. At least, that seems to be a reasonable suggestion.

Lee Everett would agree, but her husband Kenny was involved in an incident which seems to throw the question of life after death into stark focus. Whilst at a house party in Surrey, he and several others decided to play with the ouija board, not really expecting anything to come out of it. A cameraman staying with them became nervous and upset when a message came through to him from his girlfriend. She was not at the house but was, he insisted, alive and not dead as the board alleged. However, through the pointer the girl explained that she had taken an overdose and passed into the after-life that very day. Kenny Everett insists that there was no way this information could have been transmitted to anyone using the board by normal means, for they had all been together throughout the day. But shortly afterwards the cameraman decided to telephone the girl to clear the matter up once and for all. He spoke to her tearful father, who had just returned from the mortuary. Everything the board had said was true!

Was this a real message from the surviving life field of the cameraman's girlfriend? Or in the synchronistic reality which the board somehow instilled had he accessed information out of the species field and dramatized it as a final farewell from his love? At the moment we can only answer that we do not know.

12. Famous Voices from the Grave

'I had flashes in the skin and the I was out. . . The idea
to let it be. How can I put it?. . . The idea is to accept
it. . .that you're dead!' – John Lennon describing his
murder through medium Bill Tenuto.

Let us imagine that there is life after death, in some form or other.
What might it be like? From the various analogies we have drawn
in this book, and from our look at the species field and the
universal consciousness, we would probably be able to envisage
a sort of absorption into what we might call a nirvana. Our
'essence' becomes a part of the larger 'essence' which makes up
the whole of life. But how can this be any kind of continuous
existence or consciousness? How could it possibly be life as we
know it? There will be no body, no eyes, no ears, no anything –
except perhaps mind.

It is not easy, and may be impossible, for us to contemplate the
life of a mind. We might find ourselves imaging reality in the way
that we do in dreams (which also depend upon none of the
external or physical organs – except, to an extent, the brain). It
could be that our psychic faculties would come alive and we find
ourselves seeing by way of clairvoyance, hearing through
clairaudience and accessing that vast information store of
knowledge about everywhere and everywhen. Death in that case
would be rather like falling asleep and entering a never-ending
super-lucid dream. All of our experience would be in
synchronistic reality mode, and to establish contact with
somebody in normal reality (i.e. alive) might be very hard. The

degree of difficulty might best be grasped when we recall how nearly impossible it is for most of us to try to force paranormal events into being.

In this reality we cannot normally bend metal or read minds. In srm (with which death is probably concerned) it would equally be a paranormal event to hold a conversation with someone here. Normal and paranormal are relative things. They differ according to the reality mode you occupy.

The two reality modes are like a double-sided mirror. They both represent what truly is, but you cannot 'know' both at once. When you reflect yourself in one, the other is always out of reach on the far side.

Hard as it is to see how a spirit could make a conscious intervention into normal reality mode, this is sometimes claimed. For example, Charles Dickens died in 1870 with his final book, *The Mystery of Edwin Drood*, only half written. Soon after this a medium, Thomas James of Vermont, USA, began to receive urgent trance messages from the writer, explaining his desire to complete his work. The American was not a writer and had left school, aged thirteen, with little education, but he found the writing just flowing out, and he had to quit his job in order to let it do so. On 31 October 1873 the completed book was published, with an explanatory foreword 'by' Charles Dickens. The style appears to be Dickensian and maintains the use of English spellings and phraseology. Also there is no clear evidence of where the two halves join. They match well. Reviewing it, Arthur Conan Doyle said, 'The trick of thought and manner remains.'

Here we have a phenomenon similar to Rosemary Brown's music, except that Thomas James alleges no previous writing talent at all. The completion of a half-written book thanks to an apparent compulsion by its dead author does seem to hint at some element of survival, although there is no way to be sure that some aspect of James's personality did not need to pretend this and was able to do so to a paranormal degree. Or maybe it was all a clever hoax.

Doris Stokes was asked to make a deliberate attempt to contact the famous novelist George Orwell on 1 January 1984. Orwell had died thirty-four years before, leaving his black prophecy *1984* as his best-known legacy. What would he have to say about how reality matched up to his predictions? According to Doris, he felt he had been proved right, and there was a hint of bitterness in his 'voice': 'You are being brain-washed by Big Brother. It's time you said enough is enough. Computers are ruling your lives now and it will get worse. . . . You just have got to refuse to be counted.'

Supposedly Orwell gave sufficient background information to Doris Stokes, of which she was not aware, for her to be satisfied it was him. But as the whole affair was staged by an American TV company, it stands to reason that somebody present (e.g. a producer) was familiar enough with the writer for these pieces of information to be available to Doris Stokes from his life field and without any recourse to Orwell himself. In any event, these words are only what we might expect Orwell to say. There rarely seems to be much in the way of surprises care of these alleged spirits.

If you examine the countless messages that are conveyed from one side of the mirror to the other, you are sure to feel a certain disappointment. They seldom rise above a banal level stocked with platitudes. The view of 'heaven' is rather stereotyped: a sort of timeless void, with boundless space and populated by anything we care to imagine in our disembodied state as we float around (we don't have any legs to walk), feeling love and pure goodness (never badness). Actually it sounds somewhat unexciting, and one could cruelly argue that it is all a product of our limited imaginations. But it might be possible that it stems from some real after-life – and this is it!

Recently there has been a spate of books which record the experiences of people who have 'died' and then been brought back to life. There is a remarkable level of agreement, even across cultures where the religious view of life after death is widely different. For instance, upon approaching death a great sense of calmness descends. Almost nobody describes the act of death as being in any way unpleasant. Generally they then find themselves experiencing an OOBE and sometimes moving towards a bright light where they find a 'guide' to lead them on, or send them back, as the case may be.

Fascinating as this material is, it provides no evidence for life after death, for the simple fact is that *none* of these people had died, otherwise they could not have been brought back to life. Admittedly there is an enormous grey area in our science about just where death begins, but it seems fairly safe to say that at least one good definition of death is 'that state from which one does not return to life'. Consequently all these records merely tell us a good deal about the final stages of life, not the first stages of death. This may prove to be dismissing important information on a technicality. I fully accept that. According to mediums, the precise same sort of experience is reported by those who 'pass over' into the next world and do not come back. And there seems little evidence that the people who report their near-death visions were in any way familiar with the claims of mediums about those who *have* died.

Scientists argue (with some justification) that there could be any number of more realistic explanations. These visions could be hallucinations created by the drugs the person is on, or in cases where that is not true (e.g. sudden accidents) by the body undergoing a final defensive fling. Even if you accept paranormal experiences, it is not at all surprising that in a harrowing situation (where the body is full of pain or where an accident has precipitated a life-threatening circumstance) the mind might externalize itself from that body – an attempt to escape, so to speak. However, that the mind can do this when the brain remains alive constitutes no proof whatsoever that it could also do it after the brain is dead. But I have to admit that in the face of so many consistent reports these scientific explanations begin to look more and more like excuses. It may well be that we do see here the transition stage between this life and what comes afterwards.

An interesting experiment began in 1983 when a young American psychic, Bill Tenuto, began to contact the 'spirit' of former Beatle John Lennon, murdered a couple of years earlier. Tenuto is a 'direct voice' type of medium, which, as we saw before, means that he can imitate the voice of the person allegedly in communication.

Tenuto would dispute the word 'imitate'. He claims that the spirit literally takes over his body. Quite where his own spirit goes in the meantime is not made clear, but if we return for a moment to our television set analogy, we can think in terms of a video with a pre-recorded tape plugged in and overriding the normal live pictures. The signal is still 'there', although not displayed on the screen whilst the tape plays. Just how accurate or misleading this image might be is not certain. A sceptic will insist that the spirit which takes over is just another aspect of Tenuto's self, a fractionalized piece of his personality which gains the upper hand for a time. There are indeed many cases of 'multiple personality' on the records of psychologists, but these do not involve take-overs by real people, alive or dead. Still, one might say that the only reason that sort of case is not on the same psychological files is because it is on the files of psychic research instead.

Whatever the true explanation during these experiments, Tenuto's normal self certainly seems to disappear, and an entity which is at least a fair replica of the British rock star takes his place, including mannerisms, speech patterns (with frequent four-letter words!) and an accent that is like Lennon's. The effect of these things emerging through a mid-height Californian with a distinct New Jersey cadence, who in no way physically resembles the British musician, is to say the least strange.

According to the many hours of sessions which have been recorded (some of which are forming the singer's posthumous book *Little Pearls from John Lennon*), he is still a restless spirit who needs to stay fairly close to normal reality mode (or the 'earth plane' as he calls it). 'Does anyone have a bottle of beer around, or something like that?' he asks at one point. Nobody does and he remarks, 'Well, you know it's all right. It will pass. It probably wouldn't do much good for me to get a taste of it.' His desire for beer is supposedly due to the effect of inhabiting a body for the first time since his death. He has a further problem associated with this, and quickly terminated one session with the words: 'I'll tell you what I'm going to do about that. But first I got to vacate this body right now, because it needs to take a leak.'

This strange personality talks on and on about his life before and after death, and about reincarnation (because he insists that John Lennon is just the latest in a long line of incarnations on earth). I do find it midly odd that the subjects he discusses are those one might expect Americans to be interested in. He speaks much of Yoko Ono and his rivalry with Paul McCartney, but he never even mentions his first wife Cynthia or their son Julian (who worshipped his father and who has followed in his footsteps with his own musical writing in a similar vein). Cynthia and Julian were never part of Lennon's life in America and would be unknown quantities to anybody there. It does leave one suspicious of whether this omission is caused by that fact, since the medium is an American. Also, whilst the phrasing is undoubtedly English, there are occasional odd lapses into Americanisms. For instance, he says of Paul: '[He] lived in an apartment. . . . his apartment, I think, was subsidized by the government.' The habitual English way of saying that would be that Paul lived in a council flat. However, John himself spent the last decade of his life living in an apartment in America, so it is at least possible that he began to think more in such terms than in the fashion of his earlier years.

What about life in this other realm? Lennon tells us: 'I remember the feelings of things the best because they stick with you. You'll find out after you're dead . . . you don't remember the people, or the places, too well.' As for where he is – 'I never know how to answer that question, quite frankly, because first of all there is no time or space. . . .'

He is remarkably ambivalent towards his assassin, David Chapman, and claims they were acting out a drama held over from a past life where Lennon injured Chapman! 'You can't stop it if people want to shoot each other up. That's people's way of learning. It's just part of the plan.'

Looking towards the future, Lennon claims he is taking part in a grand scheme to educate mankind into the sort of realities about the synchronistic mode and life after death that we have examined in this book. 'The opportunity is now. Because if you don't do it now, in the year 1989 it's going to get worse. It's going to get very difficult beyond that in the physical.' Here he not only reflects the fears about the coming holocaust but something else I have detected from many psychic messages (be they from alleged dead spirits or from spacement): that it is necessary for psychic awareness to be triggered in as many people as possible, the real purpose of the great explosion of contact. Those who are going to see the world through the troubled times ahead will need that extra help.

Lennon claims to be working with a group of advanced souls called the 'White Brotherhood' who are using him and several people who were famous on earth (John Wayne was another of their allies. In this way they can impress the truth about the real nature of consciousness and the universe. 'People are still going to listen to me even though I am dead,' Lennon insists, and he has made a dramatic promise: 'One of me [sic] objectives is to materialize on television. I will do that. So mark it down on your little paper there.'

Whether or not there is a real surviving John Lennon there trying to fulfil this incredible stunt remains to be seen, but the sense of a real personality pervades Bill Tenuto's mediumship. Yet questions still remain. Is this marvellous acting? Does he build a pseudo-Lennon out of the data in the species field? The man was so popular and so affected that field that it has got to remain a distinct possibility. Even the echoes of our future which Lennon recites could just be Tenuto detecting bow-wave ripples and clothing them in this unusual way. They certainly have more impact because of that – which might have much to do with the subconscious reasoning.

To be honest, there is not much here that forces one into the belief that Lennon truly has come back, except the definite personality which shines through, just as Matthew Manning said it did with his artists and Rosemary Brown with her composers. Identification with the dead character to such an extent seems to me strange and needless if we are simply witnessing some form of play-acting or externalization. But then acting may indeed be the operative word. If Sir Laurence Olivier can do it, why not anybody whilst in srm? Once again we are left tantalized and uncertain.

So how would we get closer to proving life after death? Ideally we need some kind of corroboration. Hester Dowden, a medium in 1947, shows what I do *not* mean when she presented a series of automatic writings supposedly from William Shakespeare, through which she 'discovered' that his famous plays were a group effort involving Will and several other scholars. 'I was the skeleton of the body that wrote the plays. The flesh and blood were not mine, but I was always in the production,' the playwright supposedly has said. This is hardly *Romeo and Juliet*. And it is also quite useless in terms of evidence. The mystery of whether Shakespeare did or did not write the Shakespeare plays is likely to remain unsolved. And contact with the man (be he real or not) is hardly going to aid in this matter – unless he can point us in the direction of a hidden manuscript which nobody knows about. Now that *would* be interesting.

From a slightly different standpoint, we might regard multiple apparitions as significant. The Haymarket Theatre in London is said to be haunted by one of its former managers, John Buckstone. Several performers there have 'seen' him, and unlike the typical ghostly phenomenon he is not merely an image that keeps recurring in the same place doing the same thing. Buckstone turns up all over the theatre and behaves as if he is aware of the presence of his observer. That marvellous actress Dame Margaret Rutherford (who actually played the trance medium Madame Arcati in one of her most famous roles, Noël Coward's *Blithe Spirit*) had a visual apparition of him when she slept in her dressing-room. Her husband heard the sounds generated by this occurrence, as he woke from sleep, but Dame Margaret best recalled the spectre's hairy legs!

How far does this take us in terms of evidence? Some way – but there has to remain the possibility of multiple sporadic contacts with fragments of the residual life field of the old manager. Do we need to assume that he survives in any conscious sense for that to happen? I am not sure that we do, but it begs the question a little more. Ghosts which behave as if they are conscious and have personality are rare but by no means without precedent. They are extremely hard to explain in any way other than a form of survival – in which case they deserve more attention and distinction than they have hitherto been afforded.

About the closest we can get to the sort of evidence we seek is the case of Raymond Lodge, son of the famous physicist (and one of the founders of the SPR) Sir Oliver Lodge. Raymond died in the First World War trenches in September 1915 but *seems* to have transmitted evidence of his survival to his keenly interested (and therefore obviously biased) father.

Two months after his death one medium gave a message to Mrs Lodge, who had attended the session without her identity being given. (Her husband could not do this as he was too well known.) At this session there was reference to a photograph said to depict Raymond with a group of others, and specific details were offered. At the time the Lodges did not know of such a photograph, but shortly afterwards they were contacted out of the blue by the mother of an officer in the same regiment as Raymond. She had been sent a photo by her son which had Raymond on it, and she wondered if the Lodges would like a copy. Before asking for this, Sir Oliver arranged to visit a different medium and here was again treated to a description of the picture. Much more information was allegedly supplied by their dead son, including facts such as that one of the soldiers was trying to lean on him at the time and that they were 'practically' outside when the picture was taken. The Lodges compiled an account of what the photograph ought to look like and then sent for a copy. When it arrived, it was found to match the description they had extremely well, but even more interesting to me is that these details seem to have come from Raymond's point of view, looking out of the photograph, so to speak, not the way somebody looking at the print would describe them. For example, the odd remark about being 'practically' outside makes sense if you are Raymond at the place where he crouched when the picture was taken. He was in the overhang shadows of a large wooden building immediately behind him, but to a casual observer looking at the photograph that would not occur to you: you would say that Raymond *was* outside, as the different perspective (being where the photographer was and not Raymond) pushes the building more into the background.

I do not really doubt that these events are described accurately. Sir Oliver Lodge was a meticulous scientist. Of course he was already committed, but that fact would work both ways: he would have less need to prove survival, as he already accepted it. Certainly it is feasible (just about) to explain this without any form of survival, but this requires two mediums to have obtained detailed information about a photograph which at the time neither they nor the Lodges had seen, only a third party who on the first occasion was not even known about by any of those directly involved. And this information would have to be interpreted by the medium not in the way she would view the photograph (or, equally as important as the unknown third party would view it) but as if she were in the photograph (like Raymond) looking out.

Such cases (where data not known to either medium or the person to whom the message is being given later does prove to be correct) are not all that rare. They have possible explanations other than survival (generally because one can always argue that bow-wave ripples from the eventual discovery of the then unknown data are being sensed by the medium). But they much complicate the issue – perhaps too much, if you prefer to accept the simplest answer as the most likely. In such cases contact from a surviving personality *is* often the simplest answer.

Sir Oliver Lodge was also involved in what looks to be the most remarkable and probative evidence which yet exists for true survival. Barring John Lennon's promised after-death television appearance, it represents one of the most amazing feats we might expect the 'spirits' to achieve. That it would appear to have involved a sort of masterplan between three of the Society for

Psychical Research's founders is surely no coincidence. All three were classical scholars: Edmund Gurney (died 1888), Professor Henry Sidgwick (died 1900) and Frederick Myers (died 1901). All were pioneer serious researchers into the possibility of life after death and so had clear interest in coming up with something very spectacular when they had reached the other side, which is exactly how we might describe the case of the 'cross-correspondences', as they are termed.

Between 1901 and thirty years later over two thousand scripts of automatic writing were 'transmitted' by these three men (especially Myers, who seems to have been prime mover in the idea). They went to five different female mediums all over the world: three in Britain, one in the USA and one, Mrs Alice Fleming, sister of Rudyard Kipling, in India. Alice Fleming received her first Myers script in 1903. He gave her the address in Cambridge of a Mrs Verrall, and a sort of letter of introduction to the chain of mediums. Mrs Fleming had never heard of Mrs Verrall before.

As Myers supposedly put it early on to Mrs Verrall (a classics teacher at Cambridge University and the focus of the project), 'Record the bits and when fitted they will make the whole. . . . I will give the words between you. Neither alone can read but together they will give the clue. . . .' In other words fragments of a message would be received by one medium, and other fragments by one or more of the remaining women elsewhere in the world. The time delay would often preclude any possibility of collusion in the days before telephones and aircraft. But in any case on their own these fragments meant nothing; pooled together, by Mrs Verrall or the SPR, they made sense. The only hypothesis one could fall back on outside the realms of survival was an incredible form of telepathic link between the women which went on and on and was far superior to anything seen before or since, especially as the women were mostly not acquainted with one another. However, the marvellous and devious plot even served to avoid that escape route. Aside from Mrs Verrall and her daughter (who also got messages), none of the women had any knowledge of or interest in the classics, yet the messages were usually filled with allusions to them. Mrs Verrall was supposedly chosen because of her knowledge so she could decode the incoming messages and complete the ingenious pattern, but what the other women got was essentially nonsensical to them, making it hard to believe that they had been capable of picking this up by some subtle internal link with Mrs Verrall.

It is difficult to express the complexity of this mammoth project, but the situation often went something like this. Medium A would get a series of words, then medium B (without being aware of this) would get a quotation from some book or poem which contained those words; finally medium C would receive a message which on its own was just gibberish but, when put together with the first two scripts, clearly linked them together. The solution to the puzzle often came much later, when it was all figured out. The three dead spirits supposedly made it hard on purpose, to reduce the impact of those who cried fraud. Otherwise it would have been logical to make the connections less obscure and easier to spot. And it is even doubtful that some of the women would have been able to perpetrate (especially for so long) a trick such as this on things they did not comprehend.

When an American researcher called Dorr decided to test the system, he asked the Boston medium to explain the word 'Lethe', and she came out with a long script with obscure references that made no sense to her. Later Sir Oliver Lodge, as agreed, put the same question to the British medium who was not schooled in the classics; neither did she know about the previous test. Her response repeated the same references and appended the name 'Dorr'!

It seems to me that there are really only two options here. I cannot think of any mundane paranormal experience which could explain these cross-correspondences (some of which have still not been figured out). Either there was some sort of gigantic conspiracy between all these people or else Gurney, Myers and Sidgwick in some way survived death and concocted this brilliant experiment. Nobody can disprove the conspiracy theory, of course, but if the women really had no classical knowledge that is a major hurdle, and it does take a lot of powerful support for the belief that these otherwise unblemished individuals should have gone to such extreme lengths to pull off this trick for no very good reason. There is no such support. Frankly I find the hoax explanation less credible than the survival theory.

This case more than anything else leaves me guessing about the prospects of survival. It still proves nothing, but that it is precisely the kind of beautiful plan you might expect such learned men to come up with after death is surely a point in its favour.

Myers and the others often expressed their frustration at how difficult it was to get their messages across. He told Mrs Fleming that it was like 'standing behind a sheet of frosted glass – which blurs sight and deadens sound – dictating feebly to a reluctant and obtuse secretary'.

It is a little strange that the five mediums (all now dead) did not extend the cross-correspondences when they 'passed over', but perhaps it was concluded that enough evidence had already been supplied. If people were going to believe they now had the support to do so. If not, no amount of extra scripts would convince them. Myers himself communicated to Matthew Manning almost half a century after the plan had ended. He explained that the problem of survival was so complicated that nobody living could ever really grasp it. However, he did urge the young psychic to go on seeking for the answers, and then seems to have expressed his disappointment at the limited achievements of his grand experiment by adding, 'If you find [out], no one will believe you anyway.'

But perhaps the best epitaph for this whole confusing and muddling business of life after death comes from the husband of Mrs Verrall. He died in 1912 in the midst of the cross-correspondences and briefly joined in the project to remark, 'This sort of thing is more difficult to do than it looked.' We might well say that of our efforts to get to the truth about these strange phenomena.

Conclusions

Buddy Greco, the American singer, had an interesting but terrifying experience when he played a summer date on the Atlantic coast.

Relaxing on the beach, by a sea that was pretty choppy, he heard screams for help far off shore. As he was an excellent swimmer, he stripped off his jacket and plunged into the water, knifing through it in search of the source of panic. Vaguely he was aware of a boat being launched to join in the rescue, but he was well in front and half way to the stricken swimmers before the coastal rescue team were afloat. It was two girls. He could see and hear that much. Eventually he reached one of them, stopped her struggling and pushed her close to the oncoming boat, making sure they had seen her. Then he plunged deep into the water again, seeking the now ominously quiet second girl. But something hit him on the head. The rescue boat, perhaps assuming he was in trouble, had thrown out an oar, and instead of landing in the water nearby, it had struck him. He was semiconscious and fast going under. Water filled his mouth and lungs. Buddy Greco was drowning.

And then suddenly he felt a hand grab him and lift him clear of the water. He was alert enough to keep calm and did not struggle, just coughing and spluttering out the water and gulping in large doses of air. His senses returned and the hand let him go. Now he turned round to clamber onto the boat, because he knew they were so far out at sea that this was the only place from where his rescue could have come. But the boat was not there. It was well across the water, circling and seeking the missing girl. Sadly she was later found dead, but the first one had been saved by the bravery of Greco with help from the lifeguards. Greco himself had also been rescued. But by whom? He was convinced it could not be by a human.

Here we see the sort of paradox we have confronted in this book. What did save the drowning singer? Was it a physical intervention into this world by some force or entity living on the 'other side'? Or, as we saw right at the beginning of our search, with Tommy Steele's dramatic recovery from death, had Greco somehow saved himself? Had he called upon those inner resources in the deeper levels of his mind and externalized the self-help as a mystery saviour? It would not be the first time such a thing had happened.

This story is but one of many which could be told. And they will always continue to occur, because mankind is still climbing the hill of discovery. At each pause in our progress we believe we have reached the summit, but there is another peak awaiting us beyond the next rise. So it is with our knowledge of the way the universe works. We think we know it all, and yet we are probably not even half way there. The science of the year 2085 will be almost unrecognizable to us. But for those who think about the anomalies of this world, our great mysterious phenomena, the prize is a sort of sneak preview of things which one day will be as commonplace as electricity. Tomorrow they will be taught to children in every school; today they are taught only to much older children *when* they are prepared to cast aside their prejudices.

As I compiled this final chapter, I knew that I would not have to wait very long before something happened, somewhere, to someone who was famous. A strange event would baffle some personality's life and set them wondering. Of course, it did.

On 7 November 1984 round-the-world yachtsman Chay Blyth was sailing past Cape Horn with crewman Eric Blunn, fighting freezing seas as they tried to set up a further sailing record. Suddenly a huge wave struck them and they were cast into the hostile waters as their trimaran overturned. Rescue seemed unlikely as they sheltered themselves as best they could on the floating hull. The only thing which kept them going was the thought of their families seven thousand miles distant.

At the precise time this disaster struck, Maureen Blyth, Chay's wife, was at a restaurant in her home town of Liskeard, Cornwall. Suddenly the plate of food in front of her became inedible. 'I couldn't touch it,' she explained. 'I had a strange, powerful feeling. I knew something had happened to Chay.' Twenty-six hours later a Chilean ship pulled the two gallant men from the water with only minor injuries.

There was talk of a 'premonition'. In fact this is quite wrong. Maureen previewed nothing. What this demonstrates is how two life fields that are closely harmonized (as husband and wife often are) can share an event which mutually effects them in the species field. Chay's anguish impressed itself upon that field, and Maureen, temporarily entering synchronistic reality mode, was instantly aware of the emotional ripples which this created. She did not know exactly what had happened, but that is understandable: the essence of such ripples is emotion. This is what she *felt*.

The experience which the Blyths had is one of the most common in psychic records. Comedian Michael Bentine, himself a remarkable psychic, told the *Daily Mail*: 'He sent out a distress signal and she picked it up.' That is a nice way of describing it, although it is probably more correct to say that the change in his life field disturbed the species field, and because Maureen was at that time so emotionally tuned to both these fields, the ripples which the event created triggered a change in her life field as well. This she experienced as emotion, but it seems not to have been strong enough to have relayed specific information or to have precipitated a visual externalization. That occurs less often.

There have been cases of stronger contact where Maureen Blyth might have 'heard' Chay call out to her or 'seen' his presence (probably wearing his yachting gear), or just 'known' exactly what had taken place. We have met other examples of all this kind of thing elsewhere in the book. Remember Dame Margot Fonteyn, for instance?

This points us straightaway to the heart of the discoveries which we have made. For I, like you, have been following the trail of evidence and pondering its meaning.

Every individual human being (and probably every living thing for that matter) is essentially two 'selves'. We are matter and we are consciousness. They are not the same. They interact and co-operate in order for us to 'exist'. But matter does not make consciousness, and consciousness does not create matter, although it moulds and shapes it and is clearly the dominant partner when we *choose* it to be.

Matter is, of course, our physical bodies (our arms, legs, flesh, blood, brains and so on). Fundamentally it is the atoms of which our cells and our molecules are made, plus whatever extra something it is that makes those things alive and functioning like a perfect machine.

Consciousness works through the brain, like the electro-magnetic signal which permeates the circuits and innards of a television set, and like the magnetic field which orientates the iron filings. It is what we have called the life field. The life field *is* the consciousness aspect of the entity we call a human. And like the signal (as opposed to the set) and the magnetic field (as opposed to the filings), the life field is not visible or obviously detectable, but its companion (the body) is. Yet both exist. Both are totally inter-dependent, and when they separate permanently, we go through what we term death. The body is still a body, but without its life field it is a TV set irreparably broken or not plugged in to the power source. The real magic of life has gone. But gone where? Clearly the life field must *be* somewhere after death. Energy (which in some form it must be) cannot simply vanish. It either stays as it is or changes its form. So the consciousness of ourselves must, presumably, go somewhere else when we die. This might mean to 'heaven', it might just absorb itself into the larger hierarchies of consciousness, or it may hang around, drifting through the Earth's atmosphere like an ethereal, invisible tumbleweed.

I doubt that the latter occurs. If the evidence for some kind of survival is genuine, as it may well be, the first option is feasible. But the middle road seems the safest course to presume until proved false. The atoms which made up our bodies get reabsorbed by the matter which produced them (we are indeed 'clay' in that sense, as the religions tend to say). So too do we find our life field merging into a greater sea of universal consciousness – the equivalent of a raindrop being born in a cloud, living as it plunges through the sky and finally absorbing itself into the vast expanse of water we call the sea.

Yet if this is true, do we know or experience it? It seems tempting to believe so. But how does it feel? We cannot guess. However, it is interesting to realize that the atoms which once were us do not vanish. Even centuries after our death they will continue to exist, like scattered iron filings, and will eventually recombine, perhaps into some other living organism. And so may our consciousness: one day it might re-form into a smaller unit, and that unit may permeate matter once more, and we may then be 'reincarnated'. There does not seem any logical argument against that. In fact it fits what we would expect. After all, that raindrop which falls into the sea has not 'died'. It remains a part of that sea. And all raindrops come from the sea in the first place. There is a never-ending cycle which is a sort of reincarnation process for that substance we call 'water'. If it exists for water, why should we deem it impossible for consciousness?

The cosmos is a remarkably ordered place. Whether you choose to believe that this order is imposed (by God), or simply is, there is no doubting that fact. Things tend to balance – which is important, because the world of matter has a very distinct hierarchy: from the sub-atomic particles, which themselves constitute the atoms, which combine into molecules, which are the basis for cells, which originate all organs and then creatures. The upwards spiral is evident. Each unit depends upon the units which comprise it, and each unit is itself part of a grander unit. The one fact which our magical discoveries of ordinary (mundane) science has most brought home to us is that this hierarchy of matter is seemingly infinite. We probe deeper and deeper into the atom. But from days, not so long ago, when we expected ping-pong ball like objects to *be* the building blocks of matter, we have found no such thing. The ping-pong balls are not solid. The sub-atomic and sub-sub-atomic particles are not even solid. Nowhere is there a fundamental unit. The smaller we probe, the more we just find that small is not small enough, and there is another layer of the onion to unpeel.

The same applies going in the opposite direction beyond man. Beyond man? That sounds most strange. But there *are* hierarchies in terms of matter which step up from us. Man is part of the biosphere of this planet, which is part of a solar system, which is part of a galaxy, which is part of a universe, and so on! No scientist will tell you that there cannot be a super-universe of which this universe is a mere unit, or a super-super-universe beyond that. At present levels of understanding, and in view of our findings as we probe into the atom, this is hardly surprising. Consequently, it seems to be eminently logical to propose that such a hierarchy operates in that second aspect of our selves: consciousness. For what it is worth, our studies into the paranormal support this theoretical suggestion. We have already seen how thinkers such as Jung and Sheldrake have talked about each individual life field being just a part of the species field, like millions of drops of water in a puddle. Most of our strange phenomena make no sense unless we accept that. How else did Maureen Blyth become aware of the trauma which her husband was suffering? The contact had nothing to do with the world of matter and all to do with the world of consciousness.

This second hierarchy is already quite well defined, yet not so well defined as the matter hierarchy. At an inward level (because the terms 'inner' and 'outer' are better than 'below' and 'above', which falsely imply subservience) there is the conscious self and the subconscious and unconscious, although I would argue that the innermost level, i.e. the one equivalent to fundamental matter, is the personal consciousness or the 'I' self. From here we go from subconscious to unconscious and the personal, individual life field (although these last two might be identical). Outward from here would be the species field, the planetary field (all consciousness on earth) and through intermediary stages to the universal consciousness field. This latter might, and I say this with due trepidation, be what we otherwise call 'God', just as I suspect the planetary field is the home of what we might call the 'gods' (elemental creatures or nature spirits, for example).

Naturally I do not expect to have this scheme totally accurate. I am only making what seem to me reasoned speculations based on the apparent logic of the cosmos and the evidence of our discoveries.

You will recall my comments when we looked at survival that we might regard the situation as both sides of a mirror, each of which reflects its own reality, both essential and yet different. I think that we do have a sort of *principle of the two* operating at the heart of all things. There are two types of 'self', matter and consciousness, and these represent the two realities which we have used throughout the book. Matter works on the basis of normal reality mode. Consciousness functions in synchronistic reality mode.

There are many polarities which probably link in with this same premise. For example:

Normal Reality Mode	Synchronistic Reality Mode (srm)
Matter	Consciousness
Objective	Subjective
Science	Mysticism/psychic phenomena
Logic	Intuition
Cause and effect (physical laws)	Synchronicity (its laws?)
Proof and demonstration by experiment	Belief and self discovery
Atheists	Mystics
Materialists/scientists	Psychics/creative people/artists
Facts and 'real' phenomena	Images and symbols
Strict ordered time	Loose, all-pervading time
Dominant whilst awake/alive	Dominant whilst asleep/dead
Male	Female
Astrological symbol Saturn	Astrological symbol Neptune

This is the simple explanation for why we have made so little progress in understanding what we call the paranormal, for these are functions of synchronistic reality, and we have tried to delve into them with the tools of normal reality, of which science, logic and deduction are the most often used. It is hardly surprising that a century of psychical research has only given us more questions than we had before we started. We need to recognize that there are these two quite distinct principles operating around us. Once that is achieved, we shall begin to move forward. We may find solutions to many of our problems which we never expected to be soluble by way of the 'occult'!

As we saw, most people are happiest existing in one or other reality mode. It is hard to accept both at once. But our many oracles and prediction systems make good use of that. They are instruments through which the symbolic and timeless reality of the synchronistic mode can be decoded into normal reality. There are as many systems as we care to invent. We might 'read' tea-leaves, or lines on the hand, or sheep's entrails, or whatever. All that they do is act as a sharpening focus for our own abilities. There is even a story that, when Uganda was a terror state, the nation had a fortune-telling turtle! The precise method by which its activities were used is not known, but it little matters. Sadly, as I understand it, the turtle is no more. It made the unthinkable error of many an oracle throughout the ages, and predicted the demise of the despotic ruler Idi Amin. The turtle quickly ended up as soup. But it had the last laugh. Amin very quickly lost control of the nation.

I think astrology works best of all these methods, for many reasons. It represents much more clearly the inter-relation and inter-dependence of the two hierarchies. The movements of the planets against the starry background do not rule our lives, but they act in tandem with changes in them at the srm level. Something else altogether causes both sets of events (our life pattern in srm and the planetary motions in normal reality), in the same way as, when we see a barometer read 'stormy' and go outside to find dark, broiling clouds, it is *not* the barometer that has made the weather change: Atmospheric pressure has effected the storm *and* produced the movement in the barometer.

Most of us live most of our lives concerned with matter in normal reality mode – which is quite understandable, because this is the level necessary for survival on this planet. That has to be important, otherwise (one assumes) we would not be here in the first place. Even so, when we sleep srm becomes much more important for every one of us, even the most hardened materialist. And I strongly suspect that our dreams very often contain those strange paranormal phenomena, because the paranormal is just normal in the world of synchronistic reality. Try taking a dream diary and recording in great detail your dreams at first waking and *before* you get out of bed. I think you will find if you persist long enough that several examples will occur where your dreams (in their symbolic way) demonstrate changes in the species field which affect you. In a typical week that I tried this, I obtained what might be called a 'crisis telepathy' message from my cat and a 'preview' by several hours of a minor domestic happening. In one case I just detected the ripples in the field caused by my cat's distress (trapped on a high roof) and in the other bow-wave ripples preceding ahead of an event which had emotional (although otherwise trivial) overtones.

Virtually all mysterious phenomena can be explained simply in terms of life fields, species fields and the outer levels (e.g. universal consciousness). Two related life fields can harmonize. At the simplest we just say that these two people get on (or share 'good vibrations', an intuitive expression which comes close to the truth, as many of our expressions often do without conscious realization). Beyond that, they could experience empathy (a sharing of feelings) or even the embodiment of these in more concrete images (what we call telepathy). And when one of them gets in trouble and disturbs the species field, the other can immediately detect these changes (thus having a 'crisis telepathy' encounter).

But time at the level of synchronistic reality is much more flexible (if it exists at all), and bow-wave ripples (and their opposite counterpart) preceding and echoing long after events are both possible. The changes these create in the species field can also be detected and give rise to various phenomena we have met. Information from the past can be absorbed and experienced in several ways: detecting feelings, especially tragic or evil ones (we call that a 'presence' or more graphically a 'ghoul'), and picking this up in more concrete terms (as with telepathy), when we perform psychometry or, in more extreme cases, medium-ship. When we do the same thing with information about the 'future', this can again just be as feeling (a presentiment or sense of impending doom) or in more concrete images, as a prediction.

All of these things are very similar and only depend upon *where* the information comes from, e.g. another life field, the species field, universal consciousness, plus whether it is an event translated into normal reality terms as present, past or future. We can draw up a kind of matrix to show this. Read the time downwards and the source of information across to see how we name that type of paranormal experience felt by our own life field:

Source: PAST		PRESENT	FUTURE
Our own life field	Cryptomnesia (Reincarnation?)	Feelings Emotions	Intuition
Another life field	Psychometry (Medium/spirits)	Telepathy (Crisis vision)	Precognition (Future vision)
Species field	Presence (Apparition)	Invention/ creation/ discovery	Time-slips into the future

I have not considered what might lie in the boxes for planetary or universal levels of consciousness – not because I have no ideas but simply because I want to explore these further some other time. But it may be that UFOs and visits from spacemen have something to do with information obtained from the universal consciousness (past, present or future), or they could be future data from the planetary field (we may *build* real UFOs one day, that is).

, In the list above we have met all of the phenomena discussed, except timeslips into the future. This is a relatively rare experience, exemplified by Air Marshal Sir Victor Goddard who, when flying, once suddenly found himself over a strange airfield with weird aircraft. Later events seem to demonstrate this as a strong vision of how that airfield *would* look a few years on from the time when Goddard was actually flying. He had obtained information from the future of the species field and dramatized it.

The use of brackets in the matrix above is for a situation where the information is not just detected by the life field of the person in srm but *used* to override normal perception and create a vision.

A piece of information from the past of a species field, detected at a certain location, for example, might just be sensed as a feeling or presence, or it might be turned into a visual image by the mind and overlaid onto the world. It may even replace their view of the world. We then have an apparition: a dramatization of the information received. This override occurs by way of what we called a Quasi-Conscious (or QC) Experience. The mind steps down its inflow of sensory information by normal channels (which we experience as the Oz Factor). It is then open to accept an inflow of information from whatever source is transmitting it. In other words, the Oz Factor demarks the onset of a QC Experience which means that the mind is now operating in, or using data collected from, synchronistic reality mode.

Our spectrum of reality shows that the QC phenomenon is about sixty per cent objective and forty per cent subjective. So it is interpreted by us as basically *real*, yet with *dream-like* overtones. The lucid dream (of which this is a sort of mirror image) has sixty per cent subjective and forty per cent objective features. So it is interpreted by us as basically a *dream* and yet with *real* overtones. These sixty/forty figures are only guesses at this stage and should be treated as guidelines, no more. Yet they illustrate the point I wish to make.

We 'see' our ghosts and our UFOs during a QC Experience, which is why we could not (and never should) try to persuade somebody that what they saw was not really there. The fact that nobody else saw it, or perhaps just one or two other people (also operating in srm at the time), is no justification for such an argument. Yet whenever a strange phenomenon is accepted, it becomes a norm within the species field and begins to take on a sort of reality. It is then a habitual pattern of observation for somebody entering synchronistic reality. But more than that, because it can start to adopt a few characteristics of normal reality too. It's almost as if, by turning into a norm, the level of objectivity is increased and the subjectivity decreased (to perhaps seventy and thirty per cent respectively). In this way some ghosts can be photographed and some UFOs can leave physical evidence. But it is no use asking where they 'go' to afterwards, for their quasi-reality is never permanent. They are like certain kinds of sub-atomic particles, real for a short period of time when some process creates them but quickly returning to potential reality after that.

If we observe the UFO phenomenon carefully, we can see that it goes through phases. A certain novel type of report will occur and then it will simultaneously or very rapidly be observed in a number of diverse locations. For instance, in the last few years British researchers have noticed with puzzlement that we are suddenly getting a large number of encounters between UFOs and aircraft. Why has this only just begun and in such profusion? Are the aliens undertaking a new study project into British airlines perhaps? I doubt it. So what is the explanation? It is probably akin to the 'time is ripe' pattern we found, where several people come up with the same discovery at the same time. Something which makes a mark in the species field is potentially accessible to quite a few of us. It is understandable that there might not just be one person entering srm who gains this insight or has this 'encounter'. It will be a trend or vogue, but it will have some dependence upon the individual psychology of the people involved and so we shall see only a general pattern, or wave, of similar experiences, not identical reproductions. As we saw, this sometimes takes the form of psychic parallelism. For one person the information may be super-imposed onto normal reality to produce a QC Experience; to others it may be sensed at a more subtle level and used as the basis for art or creativity.

But what can we say about purpose and free will? If we foresee some sort of future disaster, can we prevent it? I certainly hope so. And I have mooted ideas about using computers on some vast project to try to correlate incoming intuitions, artistic scenarios, dreams and real visionary predictions of whatever is to come. I hope that in this way we can learn to control our own destinies a little more. For which we at least have the precedent of the phenomenon of prescripts into 'coincidental' situations. At this level we *do* see shaping of our future by our own minds in synchronistic reality mode. So perhaps it can occur on a grander scale with macroscopic events.

However, we must not be too optimistic or believe it to be that easy. An interesting case shows this. In 1981 British Rail received a call from a woman claiming to be a psychic who said that she had just had a vision in which she had seen a freight train involved in a fatal crash. Her visualization was so clear and vivid that she even saw the number of the blue diesel engine – 47 216. British Rail were, not surprisingly, sceptical, although they did have a freight engine with this number. When they checked out the woman's story with the local police (one presumes to ascertain if she was harmlessly potty or more dangerous!), they learnt that, just as she had claimed, the police did have several records of bona-fide predictions made by her.

Officially British Rail could not be seen to take the prediction seriously. Yet two years later the accident occurred in Lincolnshire exactly as predicted. A blue diesel hauling oil tankers hit a cross-country railcar, and a young girl died. The details matched the offered prediction in every detail but one: the freight engine in the smash was number 47 299.

However, train-spotter Howard Johnston, who lived near where the engine was based, had due reason to be astonished, for he had noticed engine 47 216 renumbered as 47 299 in December 1981, almost two years exactly before the accident. He was puzzled by this because 47-class diesels were usually only renumbered above 500 after major modifications. 47 216 had *not* been modified and had just taken over the number of an engine that had been. When he had inquired at the depot why this strange action had occurred, he was told about the prediction and informed that they had no intention of taking any chances! Since 47 216 was supposed to crash, altering its identity to 47 299 ought to avert the disaster.

Sadly this seems to have been a dismal failure to cheat fate. British Rail, whilst admitting the story was correct in the details above, said that they had officially logged it all as an 'amazing coincidence'. That sort of attitude is only too familiar, but what does this tell us about the value of prediction? The engine was the same and it still ran its schedule. The new number was a camouflage job, nothing more. Yet why did the premonition visualize the train as it was numbered in 1981 and not as it would be numbered in 1983? And was there any way the prediction could have rescued the train? If the engine had been taken out of service, would the crash have happened later, when it was back in action?

Obviously there are still many things we do not understand about these weird phenomena.

Another example is the very strange haunting of the set of the hugely popular American TV series *Dallas*. This saga of a Texas oil dynasty was devastated by the death of actor Jim Davis (who played 'Jock Ewing', the kingpin of the family). Yet it seems that he has not left the series after all. His apparition has been seen regularly by members of the cast, and others working around them. A Hollywood photographer saw the apparition by a swimming pool where filming was later to start. 'I know what I saw that incredible day,' he insisted. Actress Linda Gray (who plays 'Sue-Ellen Ewing') and Patrick Duffy ('Bobby Ewing') confirm some of the strange incidents, including the mysterious self-straightening photograph. This portrait of Jock continues to appear in the series, and when Jim Davis was alive, he would always make sure it was not crooked. The same thing apparently still takes place, by an unseen hand, even today.

But it was Barbara Bel Geddes, who played Jock's wife in the show until her retirement, who had the closest sighting, and the weirdest. At a time when through ill health she was struggling to make any episodes at all, she 'saw' his face reflected in a window. Thinking it might be a reflection of his portrait, she turned round. It was not. The face of Jock then smiled and said, 'You can do it if you hang in there because the kids need you.' 'Kids' was an expression he often used to describe the predominantly much younger cast.

Jock's apparition has apparently been seen in several other places too. He is always smiling and is regarded as a very happy haunting. There is much speculation about the possibility that he may be trying to make an appearance whilst a scene is actually being shot. I wonder how that would get written into the twists of the plot! But it would certainly help boost the ratings in *Dallas*'s battle with the rival show *Dynasty*. A spook is one thing the

Carrington family do *not* have!

When dealing with strange phenomena, one always needs to be cautious. I do not pretend that I can prove to you that all the events described in this book actually took place. Sometimes I venture my suspicions. On other occasions you have to remember that people in the entertainments business love to entertain, and that the media also enjoy spinning yarns which need not necessarily bear more than a passing resemblance to the truth. You are at liberty to use that as an excuse to dismiss from consideration the ideas and speculations I have offered in this book. The choice, as always, will be yours. But if I am right, and I think I must be some of the way, eventually you will confront a situation that will force you to reconsider your scepticism. That challenge to the way you view the universe may not happen today or next week, but it could. The paranormal might become real for you at any moment. I hope that, if it does, you will tell me about it. (see p. 169).

On the other hand, mankind in a broader sense may find the true facts about our twin reality forced upon it by a major, perhaps unstoppable event waiting out there for us to catch it. I do suspect that this day is coming, and coming soon, and I hope that in some small way I am helping to prepare us all to cope with that time of understanding.

I said earlier that we may observe something like a sea-change in the species field or planetary consciousness. If that happens, there are two ways you can react. You may fight the new currents but face the danger of getting swept away, or you may drift with the tide towards some new horizon. I find drifting much nicer than fighting the current. It is a practice I would strongly recommend. Take a tip from 'Luke Skywalker': let the force be with you.

Reference Section

Questions are gently probing feelers
Which reach out and fondle the dark

Answers come only to believers
Who open themselves to the spark

Any readers who themselves have experienced anything unusual and would like to convey this to the author may do so (in confidence if desired) c/o 8 Whitethroat Walk, Birchwood, Warrington, Cheshire WA3 6PQ.

The following organizations and publications are recommended for further study:

ASSAP (Association for the Scientific Study of Anomalous Phenomena), 30 South Row, London SE3 0RY.

ASSAP is open to any bona-fide enquirer and conducts research and field studies. It publishes a regular flow of magazines and reports and in combination with Aquarian Press, UK, is publishing a series of books titled *The Evidence For—*.

169

Titles published in 1983 and 1984 are *UFOs, Visions of the Virgin, Bigfoot, Alien Abductions, Phantom Hitch-hikers* and *Bermuda Triangle*. Many others are planned.

BUFORA (British UFO Research Association), 30 Vermont Road, London SE19 3SR.

BUFORA is Britain's premier UFO society, staging lectures and conferences, conducting research and field studies and publishing a range of magazines and reports. It has close contacts with bodies throughout the world and will direct any international enquiries.

Both the above societies have extensive files which are available to researchers.

Bibliography and Discography

FATE: 500 Hyacinth Place, Highland Park, Illinois 60035, USA.

Monthly and available on subscription or news-stands in the USA and in major UK stores. Popular articles on mysterious phenomena and psychic phenomena, often by established and serious researchers.

Fortean Times: 96 Mansfield Road, London NW3 2HX.

Quarterly bumper publication crammed with articles, news reports and data updates on all the latest enigmas which have been collated from a team of people all over the world. It also happens to be witty and very funny.

International UFO Reporter: PO Box 1402, Evanston, Illinois 60204, USA.

Founded by Dr. J. Allen Hynek, it is probably the world's main UFO magazine. Published bi-monthly with detailed reports on the latest key cases.

Zetetic Scholar: Department of Sociology, University of Michigan, Ypsilanti, USA.

Two issues a year, each the size of a book! Contains on-going debates between leading researchers in the paranormal throughout the world. Selects themes each issue for in-depth discussion. Eminently scientific, often sceptical.

The part-work series *The Unexplained*, published by Orbis, London, ran between 1980 and 1983 and in 156 issues contained a major documentation of the world's mysteries. The issues are likely to be reprinted and sold widely from time to time but are being republished in book form by Orbis from 1984 onwards.

Books used in the research for this work:

Arnold, Larry, *The Three-mile Island Disaster* (psychic predictions thereof) (Private, 1983)
Blackmore, Dr Sue, *Beyond the Body* (Granada, 1983)
Cheetham, Erika, *Prophecies of Nostradamus* (Corgi, 1973)
Collins, Doris, *A Woman of Spirit* (Granada, 1983)
Conan Doyle, Arthur, *The Coming of the Fairies* (Hodder & Stoughton, 1922)
Cooper, Henry, *13: The Flight that Failed* (Angus & Robertson, 1973)
Devereux, Paul and Thompson, Ian, *The Ley Hunter's Companion* (Thames & Hudson, 1979)
Dixon, Jeanne, *My Life and Prophecies* (Bantam, 1970)
Donaldson, Stephen, *The First & Second Chronicles of Thomas Covenant* (six novels) (Fontana, 1977/1983)
Evans, Hilary, *Intrusions* (Routledge & Kegan Paul, 1982)
Evans, Hilary, *Visions, Apparitions, Alien Visitors* (Aquarian, 1984)
Eysenck, Dr H. and Sargent, Dr C. *Explaining the Unexplained* (Weidenfeld & Nicholson, 1983)
Fiore, Dr Edith, *You Have Been Here Before* (Sphere, 1980)
Fisher, Joe and Commins, Peter, *Predictions* (Sidgwick & Jackson, 1981)
Forman, Joan, *The Mask of Time* (Corgi, 1982)
Grant, Joan, *Time out of Mind* (Barker, 1956)
Harrison, Peter and Mary, *Life before Life* (Futura, 1983)
Haynes, Renée, *The Society for Psychical Research* (Macdonald, 1982)
Inglis, Brian, *Natural and Supernatural* (Hodder & Stoughton, 1977)
Jung, Dr Carl, *Flying Saucers: A Modern Myth* (Routledge & Kegan Paul, 1977).
Jung, Dr Carl, *Synchronicity* (Routledge & Kegan Paul, 1977)
Keatman, Martin & Phillips, Graham, *The Green Stone* (Granada, 1984)
Kleiner, Dick, *ESP and the Stars* (Grosset & Dunlap, 1970)
Kubler-Ross, Dr Elizabeth, *On Death and Dying* (Tavistock, 1970)
Lucas, George, *Star Wars* (Sphere, 1978)
Manning, Matthew, *The Link* (Corgi, 1974)
Manning, Matthew, *The Strangers* (W. H. Allen, 1978)

Michell, John and Rickard, Bob, *Phenomena* (Thames & Hudson, 1977)

Moss, Peter and Keeton, Joe, *Encounters with the Past* (Sidgwick & Jackson, 1979)

Parrott, Ian, *The Music of Rosemary Brown* (Regency Press, 1978)

Plummer, Peter (in Davis, Richard), *I've Seen a Ghost* (Granada, 1980)

Reiff, Dr Robert, and Scheerer, Dr Martin, *Memory and Hypnotic Age Regression* (IUP, 1959)

Schatzman, Dr Morton, *The Story of Ruth* (Penguin, 1982)

Screeton, Paul, *The Ballad of Marianne Faithfull* (Private, 1983)

Seymour-Smith, Martin, *The New Astrologer* (Sidgwick & Jackson, 1981)

Sheldrake, Dr Rupert, *A New Science of Life* (Blond & Briggs, 1981)

Spielberg, Steven, *Close Encounters of the Third Kind* (Sphere, 1978)

Stokes, Doris, *Voices in My Ear* (Futura, 1980)

Van Over, Richard (Ed.), *I Ching* (NAL, 1971)

Vaughan, Alan, *Incredible Coincidence* (Corgi, 1979)

Wambach, Dr Helen, *Reliving Past Lives* (Hutchinson, 1979)

Watson, Ian, *Miracle Visitors* (Granada, 1982)

Watson, Dr Lyall, *Super Nature* (Coronet, 1974); *The Romeo Error* (Coronet, 1976); *Life Tide* (Hodder & Stoughton, 1979)

Wilson, Ian, *Mind Out of Time* (Gollancz, 1981)

The following records were also referred to:

Every Good Boy Deserves Favour, The Moody Blues (1971, Threshold, THS 5)

The Kick Inside, Kate Bush (1978, EMI, EMC 3223)

Long-Distance Voyager, The Moody Blues (1981, Threshold, TXS 139)

Secret Messages, ELO (1983, Jet, CX 527)

Synchronicity, Police (1983, A & M, AMLX 63735)

Russians & Americans, Al Stewart (1984, RCA PK 70307)

Other books by Jenny Randles:

UFOs: A British Viewpoint, with Peter Warrington (Hale, 1979)

UFO Study (Hale, 1981)

Alien Contact (Neville Spearman, 1982); (Coronet, 1983)

UFO Reality (Hale, 1983)

The Pennine UFO Mystery (Granada, 1983)

Sky Crash, with Brenda Butler and Dot Street (Neville Spearman, 1984)

Science and the UFOs, with Peter Warrington (Basil Blackwell, 1985)

Definitions of Terms

Apparition A visual perception of something not visible to people in
    normal reality mode. A form of controlled hallucination
    dramatizing data received by non-standard means whilst a mind
    is in synchronistic reality. May be loosely termed a 'ghost'.
Automatic Writing Writing/art-work/other creative material produced by
    the subject whilst in srm. Its content does not reflect the
    organization of the conscious mind of the witness.
Bedroom Visitor An apparition encountered in the bedroom, dramatizing
    material obtained whilst the mind is closer to srm during sleep or
    semi-sleep. May take several forms not dissimilar from ordinary
    dream figures to nightmare monsters.
Collective Unconscious Another name for the species field. The deeper
    levels of mind from all individuals which overlap and create a store
    of archetypes and basic life patterns. From where morphic
    resonance operates.
Lucid Dream Type of dream in which the dreamer retains a degree of
    consciousness and *knows* he is dreaming. Between midway and
    the subjective extreme on the spectrum of experience but

predominantly subjective and not objective, hence the awareness
that it is a dream and not reality.

Morphic Resonance Ideas developed by Dr Rupert Sheldrake to explain
how biological and psychological patterns occur. An averaging-
out of the most common trend within the collective unconscious
leading to a physical or behavioural 'norm'.

Night Terror Type of bedroom visit which involves acute physiological/
psychological sensations (e.g. paralysis, tingles, buzzing sounds).
May or may not be extreme enough to include apparitional
phenomena.

OOBE Out of the Body Experience. Where subject claims to experience
himself as a mind outside the physical body, often able to see the
latter. Common at times of stress, accident, illness, death etc. May
be real in an objective sense, but more likely subjective
externalization of data obtained about outside world whilst mind
is in srm.

Poltergeist Physical (often destructive or annoying) phenomenon of no
obvious objective origin. May be a side-effect of the interaction of
life fields transformed into physical energy by the laws of
conservation of energy which operate in normal reality mode.

Psychokinesis (PK) The apparent ability to create physical actions (or use
of kinetic energy) without the use of any known physical process.
Probably akin to poltergeist phenomena, but more controlled, i.e.
transfer of srm energy into kinetic energy in normal reality.

Psychometry The ability of a subject to detect information from a residual
life field whilst in srm. May simply be relayed as information or
visions, or dramatized as mediumship in extreme cases.

Reincarnation Widespread belief that each person lives more than one
life, his spirit being reborn into a physical body according to
unknown laws. May be dramatization effect of data obtained by
subject whilst in srm from harmonizing past life fields. Or may be
awareness of previous organization of the life field before birth.

Synchronicity Theory proposed by psychologist Dr Carl Jung and
physicist Dr Wolfgang Pauli to explain coincidences, predictions
and srm; processes which make no sense in terms of cause and
effect. It argues that all units in the universe are inter-related and
inter-dependent and supports the concept of hierarchies at both
nrm and srm levels.

Telepathy Alleged ability for one mind to transfer information to another,
across time and space. Probably a case of synchronization or
harmonic resonance between two life fields.

New terms introduced in this book

Bow-wave Effect An event generates bow-wave ripples (and their opposite) in the species field. Since this is not tied to normal reality concepts of time, the bow-wave ripples can spread backwards in time (as per the view from normal reality mode). A mind, entering srm, can detect these ripples and decode an event yet to happen in normal reality.

Cultural Tracking Paranormal phenomena (e.g. UFOs) demonstrate the capacity for tracking, or mirroring, the cultural images or levels of development of the day. This illustrates their primary subjective origin. Term coined by researcher Rodney Jones.

Emotive Energy Equivalent of kinetic energy in normal reality mode which is associated with the life field in srm. Fuels emotions and other phenomena at srm level. Can on rare occasions be transformed into energy forms in normal reality. (See 'Poltergeists'.)

Life Field The srm equivalent of the body, which moulds its development and acts as a pattern. The seat of consciousness for each individual.

Norm When several life fields adopt a behaviour which is at first aberrant, it can come to take on increasing influence within the species field. Eventually it will become the norm, when it gains sufficient impact. The norm dictates standard behavioural responses and what is regarded as 'real', or focuses a curse.

OZ Factor Set of symptoms at a psychological level which serves to indicate that the subject is leaving normal reality mode and entering srm. Includes sensory deprivation and time distortion effects.

Prescript Ability of the mind at srm level subtly to influence conscious behaviour (both of subject and, possibly by telepathy, of other people). This serves to direct them into situations which take advantage of information detected about future events (in normal reality mode). The result looks like a coincidence.

Psychic Parallelism When one mind, in srm, detects information from the species field (possibly bow-wave ripples from a future event or just a developing norm) and from this creates a piece of fiction, a song, etc., whilst contemporary with this another subject in srm externalizes the same information into an experience of QC reality.

The one then appears to parallel (or predict) the other, by psychic means.

Quasi-Conscious (QC) Experience Mirror image of the lucid dream on the spectrum of reality. Between midway and the objective extreme and predominantly objective, hence it is interpreted as real by the subject. But it has strong subjective elements, which involve data obtained whilst in srm which mould his impression (or experience) of the world about him, allowing impossible things to take place.

Reality Mode There are two basic ways of experiencing reality. Normal reality mode (nrm) is objective, waking and our usual everyday manner of interacting with the world. All scientific laws here apply. Synchronistic reality mode (srm) is subjective and occurs to most during sleep but is the level at which psychics operate. Different laws apply. Normal reality is of the body. Synchronistic reality is of the mind.

Residual A life field no longer attached to physical matter. It may interact with life fields of living people who may then obtain information seemingly from the past.

Species Field Another name for the collective unconscious. All the life fields of one species (e.g. man) pool themselves into this. It contains all the experience of the species. (Planetary and universal fields probably exist beyond.)

Spectrum of Reality A blending of reality experiences from objective, waking (nrm) reality at the one extreme to subjective, unconscious (srm) reality at the other. In between are different shades of phenomena, e.g. dreams, hallucinations, lucid dreams and QC Experiences.

The Force Concept coined by George Lucas to describe the ultimate field (at least the species field, probably an outer level). Can be manipulated by a subject to his own ends, either positive or negative (good or bad). The Force itself is neutral.

Index of People

Paranormal Experiences
involving:

General Index

Index of Professions

Paranormal Experiences
  involving: